S0-BNG-239

THE FIELD SPANIEL

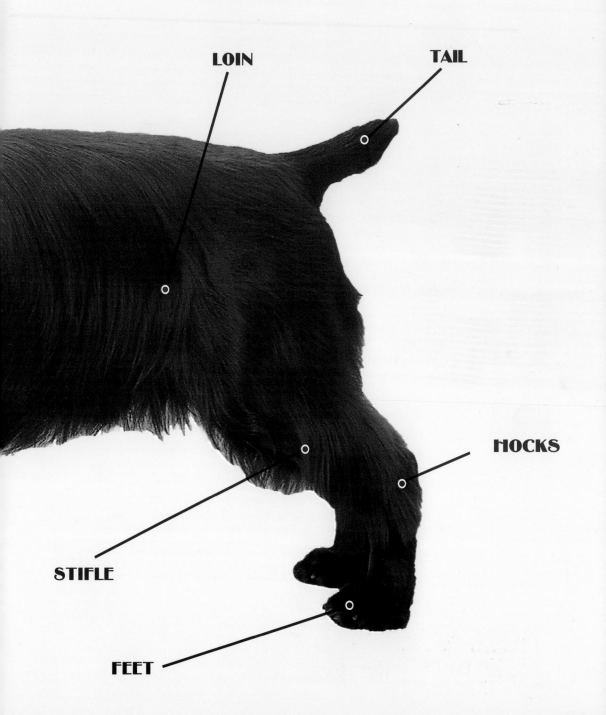

LOIN

TAIL

HOCKS

STIFLE

FEET

Facing Page: Evans' Wood Duck owned by Sarah W. Evans.

Photographers: *Susan Bartlett, Cheryl Benedict, Bob and Marcia Bengen, Agnes Clare, Sharon Douthit, Sarah W. Evans, Lynn Finney, Isabelle Francais, Karen Gracz, Eileen Griffin, D. Kay Klein, John Marx, Win McCann, Sheila Miller, George and Dorothy O'Neil, Cynthia Pischke, Maxine Reed, Frank Wolkenheim.*

© **by T.F.H. Publications, Inc.**

Distributed in the UNITED STATES to the Pet Trade by T.F.H. Publications, Inc., One T.F.H. Plaza, Neptune City, NJ 07753; distributed in the UNITED STATES to the Bookstore and Library Trade by National Book Network, Inc. 4720 Boston Way, Lanham MD 20706; in CANADA to the Pet Trade by H & L Pet Supplies Inc., 27 Kingston Crescent, Kitchener, Ontario N2B 2T6; Rolf C. Hagen Inc., 3225 Sartelon St. Laurent-Montreal Quebec H4R 1E8; in CANADA to the Book Trade by Vanwell Publishing Ltd., 1 Northrup Crescent, St. Catharines, Ontario L2M 6P5 ; in ENGLAND by T.F.H. Publications, PO Box 15, Waterlooville PO7 6BQ; in AUSTRALIA AND THE SOUTH PACIFIC by T.F.H. (Australia), Pty. Ltd., Box 149, Brookvale 2100 N.S.W., Australia; in NEW ZEALAND by Brooklands Aquarium Ltd. 5 McGiven Drive, New Plymouth, RD1 New Zealand; in Japan by T.F.H. Publications, Japan—Jiro Tsuda, 10-12-3 Ohjidai, Sakura, Chiba 285, Japan; in SOUTH AFRICA by Lopis (Pty) Ltd., P.O. Box 39127, Booysens, 2016, Johannesburg, South Africa. Published by T.F.H. Publications, Inc.

MANUFACTURED IN THE
UNITED STATES OF AMERICA
BY T.F.H. PUBLICATIONS, INC.

FIELD SPANIEL

A COMPLETE AND RELIABLE HANDBOOK

Becki Jo Wolkenheim

RX-120

CONTENTS

ACKNOWLEDGMENTS

Many thanks to the subscribers of the Field Spaniel e-mail list whose careful reflections and lively discussion of the draft versions of the manuscript contributed greatly to the overall quality of the content.

Riverly Fatal Attraction, owned by author Becki Jo Wolkenheim, is the daughter of the top stud Field Spaniel of all time in the US, Ch. Lydemoor Leslie.

HISTORY OF THE FIELD SPANIEL

That the Field Spaniel was always a manufactured breed is a statement attributed to a prominent breeder of the early 1900s. The Field Spaniel was envisioned by the earliest developers as a solid black spaniel. This was at a time when solid black spaniels were not preferred by sportsmen since patches of white in the coat made it easier to identify a dog working the field. Once upon a time, spaniels were kept primarily for working purposes. There was certainly an adequate supply of working spaniel-types to fill the needs of hunters, so the question is, why was there a need for a new spaniel breed? Quite likely, the advent of the dog show may well be the reason for the initial effort to develop the Field Spaniel as a separate and distinct spaniel breed. History shows that the dog show on a organized basis came into being at about the same time as the emergence of the Field Spaniel as a breed. As the color black had never previously been a large factor in the evolution of the spaniel, a large solid black spaniel was thought to be the means to dazzle those who judged the dog show.

The Field Spaniel emerged from dogs of rather unremarkable names such as Old Bob, Flirt, Nellie, Bebb, Fan, and so forth. Many of these animals have no particulars listed in the Kennel Club books about their lineage. The foundation stock from which the Field Spaniel developed is intertwined with the foundations of other spaniel breeds such as the English Cocker Spaniel, Sussex Spaniel, and English Springer Spaniel. The Kennel Club stud book shows that through approximately 1885, most spaniel gundog varieties were recorded as either "Land" or "Water" spaniels; those classified as Land Spaniels were equally as often called Field Spaniels. Shortly thereafter, when further distinctions between the spaniel breeds were made, it was not unusual to see Field Spaniels at working trials run side-by-side with their littermates who were registered as English Springer Spaniels, English Cocker Spaniels, or Sussex Spaniels. In particular, the common base of the Field Spaniel with the English Cocker Spaniel is emphasized by the fact that the two breeds were divided primarily by weight until 1901. Up until that time, solid-colored animals larger than 25 pounds were recorded as Field Spaniels, while those smaller than 25 pounds were recorded as English Cocker Spaniels.

Originally, the Field Spaniel's ancestors were kept primarily as working dogs by sportsmen. Ch. Woodrun's Yesterday owned by Karen Gracz.

Following the initial development as a separate breed of spaniel, the Field Spaniel suffered much at the hands of the fanciers. The natural beauty of the breed made it especially attractive to those who would set about to improve it. As a result, the Field Spaniel was bred to become a dog so long and so low as to be virtually useless in performing the tasks of a gundog. It was an aberration of type that removed the Field Spaniel far away from the original visions of the early developers. The general public was not impressed and turned away from this lovely utilitarian breed, and the Field Spaniel has never again regained his original popularity. The extreme version of the breed, that contributed heavily to the near demise of the Field Spaniel, was a dog with a very long back, crooked legs, beautiful yet heavy head, and excessive feather. By the 1920s, one English author penned, "The Field Spaniel is down and has taken the knockout. They were wonderful creatures, which have been likened to cucumbers, caterpillars and other elongated and unsymmetrical forms of still and active life. They had beautiful heads, and crooked legs. They were as long in the back as a little village and their couplings showed a hiatus between the back rib and the stifle that would not have disgraced a Dachshund or Basset."

These physical traits were the result of outcrosses, most notably to the Sussex Spaniel. Evidence also exists for the introduction of Basset Hound in approximately 1880, reportedly to acquire additional coat color variations as well as to shorten the leg. The show ring wins accumulated by this exaggerated type of Field Spaniel certainly contributed to the perpetuation that of type. Records show that judges often compared the Field Spaniels of the time side by side in an effort to determine which dog was the longest and lowest to the ground. While it is easy to place the blame for the near ruination of the breed on breeders perpetuating this type of Field Spaniel, it is somewhat unjust. At the time, there was also a pervasive theory among sportsmen that a low-set spaniel would work thick cover more effectively than one with relatively longer legs. In addition, it was thought that the lower stationed spaniel would out of necessity be slower of pace, work closer to the hunter and be easier for the foot hunter to follow. The Basset Hound outcross, in addition to producing the lower-stationed animal with more coat color variation, was likely an attempt to improve the "nose" or scenting capability of the breed important for a working hunter.

Following the extreme exaggeration of type produced early in the 1900s, the breed went into a demise. Finally saved by fanciers who had the good sense to preserve and restore the original type envisioned by the developers of the breed, further outcrosses to the English Springer Spaniel prior to and once following World War II were made to restore a more upstanding type of dog.

All modern Field Spaniels descend directly from two dogs and two bitches; every line of every pedigree eventually leads back to one of the four. This point is important to remember since even today the genetic base of the breed is extremely narrow.

Two dogs, Ronayne Regal and Gormac Teal, both black in color, were littermates whelped in 1962. They were the first registered as "pure" Field Spaniel by the Kennel Club following an outcross to the tri-colored English Springer Spaniel Ch. Whaddon Chase Duke in 1956. Regal figures prominently in pedigrees through his son, Ridware Emperor, and his daughter, ShCh. Mittina Ridware Samantha. These were produced by Columbina of Teffont, a black bitch whelped in 1957 and one of the four foundation animals for the entire breed today. Teal figures prominently in pedigrees through siring two famous litters, the "J" litter from Mittina, two of whom came to the United States, and

The Field Spaniel has survived many crosses with other spaniel types to retain his distinctive characteristics. Ch. Woodrun's Grand Slam, UDX, owned by Becki Jo Wolkenheim.

the "A" litter from Elmbury, to which most of the more recent imports date.

Elmbury Morwenna of Rhiwlas, affectionately known as "Butty" by her owner, was a liver color bitch whelped in 1963. She is the final one of the four foundation animals to which all modern Field Spaniels date. Butty, herself, was extremely inbred as she was the product of a littermate breeding between Justice of Rhiwlas and Jillian of Rhiwlas. This breeding was important in that it contained none of the English Springer Spaniel lines from the outcross of the 1950s. Bred to Ridware Emperor, Butty produced one litter of ten from which the first three littermate Field Spaniels flew to the US and became the foundation of the breed on this side of the Atlantic.

THE FIELD SPANIEL IN AMERICA

In 1894, a liver-colored dog named Coleshill Rufus became the first Field Spaniel registered by the American Kennel Club. By 1909, the Westminster Kennel Club had a very respectable entry of nine Field Spaniels. Yet, not one of the early Field Spaniels imported to form the initial base of the breed in the United States appears in any pedigree in the world today. Always a rare breed, the Field Spaniel in the US had a blow struck in late 1909 when a fire destroyed a prominent kennel and ten Field Spaniels were lost in the blaze, including the top winners in the breed. The owner of these lamented that he would try to search for Field Spaniels to replace those he had lost but doubted that he could find their quality. This was the beginning of the decline of the breed in America. The last champion Field Spaniel of the early introduction of the breed into the US was recorded by the American Kennel Club in 1916. It would be over 50 years before another champion would be recorded. The last registration of the initial beginnings of the breed was recorded in 1930; the next registration would not be recorded until the late 1960s when three imported Field Spaniels were brought into the US to re-establish the breed from the small amount of stock remaining in England.

The modern re-birth of the Field Spaniel in the US began in the homeland of the breed in December 1966 when a litter of ten was whelped. Three of this litter were imported to America and were sired by Ridware Emperor (liver dog) out of Elmbury Morwenna of Rhiwlas (liver bitch). All carried the "Mittina" affix of

Mrs. A.M. Jones, MBE. At the time, Mrs. Jones was anxious to import Cocker Spaniels (American) from the US to establish a breeding program. In contacting two American breeders of Cocker Spaniels, a trade was arranged and paved the way for three littermate imported Field Spaniels to become the foundation for the modern revival of the breed in the US.

In January 1968, the American Spaniel Club show presented the three-year-old littermate Field Spaniels. The total entry, two dogs and one bitch, marked the dawn of the new era. All of the three Fields shown became American Kennel Club bench champions over the next two years. These Fields were: "Mac" (Ch. Pilgrim of Mittina) and "Twiggy" (Ch. Flowering

The Clumber Spaniel is one of the many distant members in the Field Spaniel's lineage. Owners, George and Dorothy O'Neil.

May of Mittina), owned by Richard and Doris Squier of Randolph, Ohio; and "Brig" (Ch. Brigadier of Mittina) owned by P. Carl Tuttle of Rectorville, Virginia. All were bred by Mrs. A.M. Jones, MBE of England and were liver in color. Adding to the memorable occasion of this show was that "Mac" and "Twiggy" were awarded the Best Brace in Show award.

In December 1968, "Mac" and "Twiggy" produced the first American-bred litter, thereby re-establishing the breed on this side of the Atlantic. This was the first litter born in the US in approximately 50 years. From this litter, the littermates "Limei" (Ch. Squier's Pilgrims Progress) and "Mae" (Ch. Squier's Mayflower), both livers, flew to Houston, Texas to become the foundation stock for the Kare-Dawn kennel.

In August 1970, Flowering May of Mittina accumulated the required number of championship points to become the first Field Spaniel champion recorded by the AKC in 54 years. Her son, "Limei" (Ch. Squier's Pilgrim's Progress, owned and shown by Sandra Burt-Jones, Kare-Dawn) later became the first American-bred champion of the modern Field Spaniel revival in the United States.

July of 1970 produced more breed firsts, as Ch. Kare-Dawn's Jenny Lynd, a liver and tan bitch bred by Sandra Burt-Jones, accumulated the required number of points to become the first-ever Canadian Field Spaniel champion. This first was soon followed as Ch. Kare-Dawn's Pancho Gonzales, CD, a golden liver and tan bred by Burt-Jones and owned by Jeanette R. Spurlock of Louisiana (Fetherfield), completed the requirements for a Canadian championship as well.

During the early 1970s, Field Spaniel fanciers were a rare and widely dispersed group. A newsletter was initiated to promote communication among the few and widely scattered fanciers. Sadly, an early issue of the newsletter included a memorial to "the first lady" of the breed, Ch. Flowering May of Mittina, who had died in late 1974. During this time, the liver bitches Ch. Joanne of Mittina (imported by P. Carl Tuttle, Gunhill Kennels) and Ch. Jeannie of Mittina (imported by Richard Squier, Squier's Kennels) were brought into the US. These were from the important British litter often referred to as the "J" litter and contributed heavily to the early development of the breed in the US.

Also during the early 1970s, Ch. Whitelench Hoity-Toity, who has been called "the dam of the color black," was rescued from a Canadian shelter by Richard Squier who also managed to obtain her registration papers. "Boots," as she was called, became the first champion of the modern Field Spaniel revival of the black coloration and was also the first Field Spaniel to place in the Group ring (1975). Even today, the majority of black Field Spaniels in the US will be noted to have "Boots" in their extended pedigree; the fortunate set of circumstances that led to her rescue has had an undeniable effect on the development of the breed in the US. By 1975, American Kennel Club statistics show that the Field Spaniel had climbed in popularity to the rank of 118 out of a then-total of 121 recognized breeds.

Mrs. A.M. Jones, MBE donated a perpetual trophy

U-AGI, U-CD Ch. Calico's Royal Flush'R, CD, NA, CGC, or "Nigel" to his friends, is the first Field Spaniel to earn an agility title. Owner, Eric Hendrikson.

for award at the annual American Spaniel Club show in 1976. This trophy, awarded for the first time in January 1977, is still awarded to the Best of Breed Field Spaniel at this show. The first winner of the Mittina Trophy was Ch. Mark Twain's Samuel Clemens, a liver dog owned by Elaine (Gribble) Bertsch and bred by the Squiers.

In 1977, Win McCann (Parma Heights, Ohio) showed the first Field Spaniel to an obedience title, the American Kennel Club Companion Dog (CD) degree. Ch. Squier's Becca Burwell, CDX, TD would later add the Companion Dog Excellent (CDX) title as well as a Tracking Dog (TD) title. Especially remarkable, Becca was under one year of age when she won her first obedience title. The record-setting AmCan Ch. Kare-Dawn's Pancho Gonzales, CD added the Companion Dog title just a few short months later, ably guided by Jeanette Spurlock (Fetherfield). Another performance milestone was achieved in 1977 as Cobble Hills Cheerio, TD sniffed his way down a track and earned the first-ever tracking dog title.

Spring of 1978 brought word via the breed newsletter of the death of Ch. Pilgrim of Mittina. On June 10, 1978, the organizational meeting of the Field Spaniel Society of America was held; 13 years later this organization became the official parent club of the breed, duly recognized as such by the American

Kennel Club in 1991. Another notable dog of the 1970s was Ch. Cobble Hills Milestandish, who for the first time in breed history won first place in Sporting Group competition and shattered previous records for the breed in the area of total dogs defeated.

The 1980s brought about further development of the breed in the United States that paralleled the development of the Field Spaniel Society of America, Inc., (FSSA). The progressive growth and maturation of the FSSA as the parent club of the breed was instrumental in bringing together a diverse group of fanciers with a single-minded goal: to protect the Field Spaniel as a distinct spaniel variety and to preserve the best classic physical features of the breed while eliminating faults in type. Efforts toward preserving both the mental and structural abilities of the Field Spaniel, along with the physical features (i.e., "type") that clearly separate the Field Spaniel from other spaniels, was and continues to be a commitment of breeders, fanciers and the parent club. One can imagine the difficulties of carrying out the duties of a club with fanciers who were so widely scattered and few in number. Indeed, by early 1979, newsletters reveal the normal growing pains of most young organizations. However, the members of the fledgling club persisted and by 1980 the first fun matches were held. These fun matches were and are a required part of the process of club recognition by the American Kennel Club. The holding of fun matches for the purpose of amiable competition and other events on an organized basis brought fanciers together and offered a venue for continued development of the breed. On June 28, 1980, 11 Field Spaniels were exhibited at the first fun match of the club. Another match soon followed on July 26, 1980, with a third held on September 13, 1980. During the 1980 year, AKC registered a total of 32 Field Spaniels.

In 1981, the American Spaniel Club held its 100th anniversary show. Fifteen Field Spaniels were shown, a respectable entry even by today's standards. Later in 1981, the first Field Spaniel Society of America supported entry show was held in Williamsport, PA at the Bald Eagle KC show on July 26th.

In 1982, national level publications noticed the breed and *Off-Lead* magazine featured a Field on the cover in March. This Field Spaniel was the first UDT (Utility Dog Tracking) titlist, Ch. Cobble Hills Poo, UDT, owned and trained by Laurie Fischer Bach of

North Carolina, bred by William Pace II also of North Carolina. *Dog Fancy* magazine featured the Field Spaniel in the April issue, including in the write-up a picture of the imported black bitch, Ch. Leeonvale's Saffron. Another noteworthy accomplishment of 1982 was the attainment of the first obedience Dog World Award by Ch. Jester's Bertschwood Bekki AmCan, UD, TD, owned and trained by Judy Byron of Ohio, bred by the Hovaneks of Ohio (Jester's affix).

Fanciers of the Field Spaniel formed a movement designed to protect the breed as a distinct variety of spaniel and to preserve his unique qualities. Ch. Kenmare Admiral Lord Nelson owned by Agnes Clare.

The club continued holding fun matches, venturing for the first time to the Southern regions of the US. Club records for the period reveal a 1982 membership of 28 households and 42 individual members. How-

ever, by the fall of 1983, newsletter records reveal a club that was faltering even as the breed continued to make record-setting firsts in dog show competition in the US. During 1983, Mark and Michelle Hovanek's home-bred Ch. Jester's Shady Lady, CDX earned the first High In Trial award for the breed from the Open A class with a score of 196.5.

By 1985, the fledgling Field Spaniel Society of America had matured into a more cohesive group of fanciers with the goal to achieve the elusive AKC recognition of the Club as the officially designated parent club of the breed in the United States. The membership of the period included 32 households spanning 15 states.

Importation of more Field Spaniels during the 1980s was especially beneficial to the continued development of the breed. These included the dogs Ch. Lydemoor Leslie (George and Dorothy O'Neil, Wicksford Kennels), Ch. Glad Tidings of Westacres (Joan and Michael Faulkner, Jeran Kennels), Ch. Muharraq Jester (Alan Conner, Terralan Kennels); and the bitches Ch. Bowgate Tepas (Faulkner), Ch. Bowgate Showgirl (Jeannine Pyles, Chambord Kennels and Richard Squier, Squier's Kennels), Ch. Bowgate Jeran (Faulkner), and Ch. Muharrao Parramatta Girl (Slattery, Cotoica Kennels). All were liver in coat color and represented some of the finest lines in England. The contribution of these imported Field Spaniels to the continued development of the breed in the US is priceless and reflected by noting that these animals may be found in the pedigrees of virtually every Field Spaniel presently winning in the dog show ring.

Toward the end of the 1980s, Field Spaniels started to achieve more notice in the show ring. One notable bitch, Ch. Jester's Bubl'N Brown Sugar (Honavek, Jester's Kennels), became the only Field Spaniel bitch to achieve the top rank for yearly statistics based on number of wins and dogs defeated, the first to gain a first place in the Sporting Group, and the top-winning bitch by virtue of group placements. Ch. Jeran's Daydream Believer (Jeannine Pyles and Clint Livingston, Chambord Kennels) achieved a record-setting 73 group placements during his show career, including a remarkable five Sporting Group wins. Of high interest is that "Derby" was shown throughout his career by Clint Livingston, then a junior handler who competed in Junior Showmanship competition during much of that time and earned the first-ever all breed show Best Junior Handler award for junior handling a Field Spaniel. The liver dog Ch. Lydemoor Leslie (George and Dorothy O'Neil, Wicksford Kennels) in 1989 defeated over 5000 dogs in Group competition. He is also the top sire of champions in breed history with 19 champions sired to date.

The decade of the '90s has been marked by a striking increase in the accomplishments of both the breed and the parent club as they continue to develop side-by-side. The anticipated licensure from the American Kennel Club was achieved and paved the way for the first national specialty show held in 1991 in Sedalia, Missouri, with annual shows held every year thereafter. Winning Best of Breed at this first-ever event was Ch. Woodspoint Jeran Martin (James and Lucille Gallagher, Shenanigans Kennels), a liver dog, while his littermate, Ch. Jeran's Waterford Crystal (Janice Masters, Briarwyck Kennels) won the Best of Opposite Sex to Best of Breed award. A top-winning dog over a period of years, "Martin" also achieved a remarkable five Best of Breed wins at the annual American Spaniel Club show, a record that is not likely to be broken for quite some time.

Ch. Squier's Clara Barton, owned by the author, shows her skill at the bar jump. She is the dam of the first obedience trial champion in Field Spaniel history — so talent must run in the family!

The Field Spaniel received even more notice in the all-breed dog show rings. Ch. Cotoica's Oxford Street owned and bred by the Slattery's (Cotoica Kennels), a liver-color son of the imports Ch. Muharraq Jester and Ch. Bowgate Tepas, finished his championship in three consecutive days of showing in late 1989. He then went on to a distinguished show career that included a national specialty show Best of Breed win in San Antonio, Texas in 1993. "Plano" has more than proven his worth to the breed in siring a number of bench champions as well, including six from one litter for Jeannine Pyles (Chambord Kennels). His littermate Ch. Cotoica's Picadilly Circus (Dottie Slattery, Cotoica Kennels) was also a group placer in the show ring, award of merit winner at the national specialty and a dam of several champions. Meanwhile, the young liver-color Ch. Bitterblue's Triple Crown, WDX earned the top honors at the National Specialty in 1992 at the tender age of 18 months shown by breeder Lynn G. Finney (Bitterblue Kennels). A grandson of the import Ch. Lydemoor Leslie, he has set a number of breed records in the intervening years. These include defeating more Field Spaniels in earning the Best of Breed award for four consecutive years, tying the previous record for total number of show career Group placements in 1996, and in doing so breaking the previous record for total number of dogs defeated in Group ring competition (shown by J. Ralph Alderfer for co-owner Helga Alderfer, Pin Oak Kennels). "Tank," as he is known, has proven the versatility of the breed as well by earning the parent-club title of Working Dog Excellent (WDX) as well as a qualification for the American Kennel Club Junior Hunter (JH) title. In addition to all of this, "Tank" regularly works as a therapy dog with his owner Sharon Deputy (Breezy Hollow Kennels).

The elusive Best in Show award at an all-breed event was earned in 1992 by the liver-color Ch. Theralan Thrills N'Chills. Sired by the import, Ch. Muharraq Jester, bred by Alan Conner (Terralan Kennels) and owned by Conner and Michael Schmitt (R-Own Kennels), "Chilly" won a second Best in Show in 1993. Along the way, "Chilly" twice earned the coveted top berth in the breed in terms of total dogs defeated in Group competition. A littermate, Ch. Theralan Ooooz N'Ahhz, CD (Sharon Shiminsky, Crystal Rose Kennels), did much to pave the way for bitches to receive notice in the Group ring as well, while showing the dual abilities of the breed by earning a Companion Dog title with class placements. A liver granddaughter of the remarkable Ch. Jester's Bubl'N Brown Sugar, "Sarah" has proven her worth in producing winning Field Spaniels as well.

Not all of the top-winners have been liver in color. The black Field Spaniel Ch. Tamoshire Midnight Rendevous (Sharon Douthit and Susan Strong) made his way into the Group rings. In doing so, "Rondy" broke the previously held record for black Field Spaniels in terms of total dogs defeated within the Group.

In the performance arenas, a number of breed firsts

have been accomplished. In 1992, the first hunting title was earned by Ch. Riverly Formal Attire, JH, WD (Elizabeth and Vera Montgomery, Riverly Kennels). The first Obedience Trial Champion (OTCh) was earned in 1993 by Ch. and OTCh. Calico's Lil Deuce Coupe, UDX (Becki Wolkenheim, Calico Kennels). "Cooper" further exemplified the versatility and keen trainability of the breed in earning a berth on the "Top 25 OTCh" dog list compiled by the American Kennel Club in 1993. A second OTCh title was earned in 1994 by Ch. and OTCh. Calico's So Fine Four-O-Nine, UDX (Becki Wolkenheim, Calico Kennels), a liver bitch known as "Chevy." In addition to earning top honors for a bitch in group competition, gaining the

Field Spaniels can excel at many activities and Albetcha's Percy Shelly is a pup full of untapped potential!

second ever Sporting Group win along the way, this liver daughter of the first OTCh bitch in breed history further distinguished the breed as keen competitors by earning a Highest Scoring Dog in Trial award, Highest Combined Score award and a Group Placement in day of competition at an all-breed dog show. Also paving the way in performance, the liver dog Ch. Calico's Royal Flush'R, CD, NA (Eric Hendrickson) has proven the abilities of the breed in agility performance competition, with several perfect scores and numerous placements en route to the Novice Agility title in 1996.

DESCRIPTION OF THE FIELD SPANIEL

The very name "Field Spaniel" is somewhat a name lacking in character for a breed that is anything but non-descript! The modern Field Spaniel satisfies both the eye of the serious show dog fancier who appreciates his physical beauty and the purpose of the hunter who desires a companion for a day afield. Males are from 18 to 19 inches at the shoulder in height and will weigh 50 or more pounds when mature. Females average 17 to 18 inches in height and corresponding with less overall height, weigh less than the males.

Best described overall as moderate and well-balanced with no exaggerated features, the Field Spaniel is at the same time renown for his beautiful head. Framed by low-set and well-feathered long ears that lay close to the sculptured skull, the head of the Field

Opposite: Ch. Wicksfords Dinah, CGC, owned by Brenda Lawry and George and Dorothy O'Neil.

Maplesugar Carrilon is a typical Field Spaniel — a hardy dog that loves to be outdoors in all kinds of weather. Owner, Becki Jo Wolkenheim.

DESCRIPTION

Spaniel at once conveys the impression of nobility, intelligence, and good nature. When viewed from the top, the skull and foreface are rectangular in shape, and together form an overall rectangular shape as well. When viewed from the front, there is just the slightest amount of widening toward the backskull, yet there is no hint of a wedge shape. A slight prominence of the occipital bone immediately at the area where the skull attaches to the neck is noticeable but is neither peaked in appearance nor protruding.

Expressive brows perch above lively, yet kind brown eyes that are somewhat widely-set. The eyes are slightly almond in shape with lids that are tightly fit. Eye color will vary from a deep hazel to a deep, dark

The Field Spaniel is a well-balanced dog that possesses a straight topline and noble features. Ch. Terralan Kayti of Waterfield owned by the author.

brown as befits the coat color of the dog. The foreface beneath the eyes is chiseled and the cheek bones are relatively flat. The muzzle is long and lean; this length of foreface is longer than that of the other spaniel breeds. The nose is set-on as an extension of the muzzle and is noticeably large, and colored brown or black to tone with the overall coat color of the dog.

The entire head is set onto an arched and strong neck of good length. The neck flows smoothly into shoulders which are sloped when the dog is viewed from the side. The front legs are set well beneath the body such that the foremost portion of the chest is easily visible. From the front view, the space between the front legs of a mature Field Spaniel should easily be as wide as the average hand width of an adult. When assessing the width of the chest, it will be noted that the breast bone readily fits neatly into a cupped hand. The entire assembly of the neck, shoulders and legs (sometimes called the "forehand") allows the legs to move fore and aft easily when the dog is on the move. There should be no choppiness or high-stepping noted when the forelegs are in action, with smooth flowing movement beginning in the shoulder to drive the legs forward with no hint of strain.

The back, or topline, of the Field Spaniel is level and held firmly whether the dog is standing still or moving and has just the slightest suspicion of length. Fanciers sometimes use the fanciful description that a Field Spaniel could carry a tray on his back, with a full glass of water and never spill a drop because the topline is so firm and level. This topline is supported by a framework of rib and muscle. The rib of the Field Spaniel is considered one of the hallmarks of the breed: when measured for length, the forechest to the end of the rib will be approximately equal to two-thirds the length of the entire dog from forechest to rear. The underline of the body gently curves into the loin without exaggerated tuck-up of the loin. At the same time, there is no tubular appearance to the body as the loin is gently differentiated. The overall depth of the body from withers to chest is approximately equal to the length of the leg from elbow to ground.

The Field Spaniel is a muscular, athletic dog that moves smoothly and rapidly over rough field and ground.

Ch. Woodrun's Grand Slam, UDX, owned by Karen Gracz, shows his prowess as a hunting dog by bringing back the game to his master.

The croup gently falls away from the topline without any tendency to an acute slant. The tail is merely an extension of the spinal column and is set on at the croup to follow the general and smooth line of the croup. As a result, the tail comes straight off the croup with a slightly downward angle. There is no concave outline at any point when viewing the croup and set of the tail. The haunches should be nicely rounded in appearance, obviously muscled and strong. The rear legs show moderate angles and are well-muscled and strong. This allows for a strong push from the rear to propel the Field Spaniel when on the move.

The feet of the front and rear legs are large and have well-arched toes that fit tightly together. The sheer size of the Field Spaniel foot is often viewed with awe by those unfamiliar with the breed. However, it is this large and well-shaped foot that allows the Field Spaniel to work in rough terrain with excellent maneuverability and stability. The webbing of the foot between the toes enhances the ability of the Field Spaniel to navigate with minimal effort when swimming. Dewclaws are generally removed within a few days of birth, as they are prone to injury that is not only painful but may result in a more complicated surgery when such injury occurs in the mature animal.

In moving, the action should appear effortless, with strides that are long and low when the Field Spaniel is in an extended trot of moderate speed. The distance of forward reach of the front leg should be complementary to the distance of backward push of the opposite diagonal hind leg in the trotting gait. Each stride should result in the Field Spaniel covering a good amount of ground. The result is the characteristic smooth free-flowing gait of the Field Spaniel. Upon observing this gait, one can readily imagine the dog continuing this pace for long periods of time while working during a day in the field. When moving, the tail of the Field Spaniel should be held parallel to the ground, without any tendency to carry the tail above the level of the back. In action, the tail should be wagging, often in a precise beat as if acting as a metronome for the strides. The tail is customarily docked to balance the overall animal. Docking the tail is generally preferred by most breeders in the US, as the full tail may be subject to injury in the working hunter. The overall length of the docked tail is generally longer than seen in many other spaniel breeds, generally from four to six inches in length in the mature animal. However, it must be noted that docking the tail is not required. Field Spaniels with full tails are being successfully shown to championship titles in the United States. As there has been virtually no selective breeding for a specific length and shape of the tail, there may be variation in the appearance of the tail of the Field Spaniel that is left undocked.

This litter of puppies demonstrates the many colors that the Field Spaniel can represent — liver, liver roan, blue roan, liver roan and tan, black and black and tan. Owner, Lynn Finney.

Proper set and carriage of the tail is more important than whether the tail is docked or undocked.

Long silky hairs lying thick, flat and close make up the Field Spaniel coat. The silky texture is important in that it is the texture that prevents burrs and other debris from entangling in the coat. The thickness of the coat is important to provide the Field Spaniel with insulating protection in the extremes of weather and prevents injury to the skin when hunting through dense cover.

The coat is seen in a variety of colors, though the Field Spaniel is considered a "solid-color" dog in that the basic color of the coat covers the entire body of the dog. The most common colors are liver and black. The term "liver" is descriptive of a brown, with a range in depth of color from chestnut to bittersweet chocolate. Other colors include liver and tan points, black and tan points, blue roan, liver roan, or either roan with tan points. Tan points refer to a tan to golden-toned color that generally appears as a small spot on the brow above each eye, the sides of the muzzle, front and rear pasterns, and around the anal region. Some descriptions of Field Spaniel color will include "mahogany" in the listing of possible coat colors; while this term may be arguably more descriptive than the term "liver" for the deep brown coat with a reddish cast, it is not a term in present day use. While Field Spaniels may also be clearly black and white or liver and white in color, with or without ticking of the darker color in the white coat of the dog, these colors are considered controversial by some fanciers. Field Spaniels of these colors are not generally seen in the conformation show ring, though history shows a small number so colored have attained championship titles. A small patch of white on the throat and/or forechest is often seen. The size of the white in these areas may have an effect on how well the animal does in the conformation show rings. There is debate about how much white is too much white among breeders, since the term used is relative, i.e., a "small amount" of white on the throat and/or forechest is acceptable. A descriptive word portrait offered by one fancier is that "a necktie of white is OK; a shirtfront is not." It must be emphasized in final analysis, however, that neither the amount of white on the throat and/or forechest nor the general overall coat color have any bearing on the abilities of the Field Spaniel as a companion in one's home.

Opposite: Although considered a "solid-colored" dog, black and tan Jody and her liver-colored friend Becca are examples of common colors in the Field Spaniel. Owner, Win McCann.

CHARACTERISTICS OF THE FIELD SPANIEL

The Field Spaniel is perhaps the most versatile of all gundog breeds. Whether you wish to have a bit of fun exhibiting at a dog show or training your dog for hunting, obedience, agility or tracking, Field Spaniels are willing participants and generally pleased to be involved in any activities their owner might wish to pursue. As companions they have few rivals, combining a healthy dose of impishness with an affectionate

The Field Spaniel is one of the most versatile of all the gundog breeds. Casey is being congratulated by owner Tom Gracz on a fine flush and retrieve.

The Field Spaniel is an affectionate, loyal dog and once he trusts and knows you, he will be your friend for life. Owners, George and Dorothy O'Neil.

nature and devotion to their owners. The breed is highly intelligent, with a penchant for instinctual problem solving. These traits are cherished by those who own them.

The very intelligence of the Field Spaniel lends itself to a reserve noted in many, though not all, members of the breed. This reticence is often seen when the Field Spaniel is introduced to a stranger. The Field Spaniel may be somewhat aloof though never indifferent upon first meetings, preferring to look over the individual before deciding if the person is deserving of his friendship. Fanciers believe strongly in a perceptive sense innate to the breed. Stories abound about specific people ignored by a Field Spaniel, despite repeated overtures, and who were subsequently proven to be untrustworthy. This reticence upon introduction to a stranger should not be confused with shyness or fearfulness. The behavior of a Field Spaniel exhibiting the natural reserve and aloofness with strangers is distinctly different than behavior generally associated with shyness. One owner offered the following description: "I think of Fields as looking a situation over for a bit before launching into it, but then they exhibit an exuberant outlook as if something wonderful is just about to happen; they don't know what, but they're sure of how wonderful it will be." Once the Field Spaniel has met and accepted a new friend, he will generally recognize the individual from there on, enthusiastically greeting his friends and soliciting attention.

Both males and females exhibit similar personality traits, though fanciers of the breed often remark that the males are more likely to be affectionate toward their owners. The females, while also sweet and companionable, are noted to be slightly more independent. In general, the breed craves human companionship, exhibiting an utmost and fervent desire to be part of every facet of their human pack's lives. Field Spaniels predictably get along well with children and other animals in the household when properly supervised.

The breed standard uses the word "docile" in its description of temperament. This is perhaps a bit misleading. The breed may be considered docile in that they are generally stable, predictable and tractable in nature, but it is a misnomer because the breed as a rule possesses medium to high energy and is animated. Field Spaniels are bred for activity and endurance. They are often described by fanciers as "busy," typically on the go, playful and interested in all events surrounding them.

The word "determined" also comes to mind when describing Field Spaniel temperament. This is not to be confused with stubbornness and hard-headedness. The Field Spaniel is relatively sensitive in that behavioral training does not require harshness; in fact, often verbal corrections are sufficient. Yet the breed as a whole is determined in that they are resolute and will persevere to reach a goal — whether that goal is finding a bird in the field or retrieving a toy in a game of fetch.

While a Field Spaniel will adapt to a kennel environment for short periods of time, maintaining the Field Spaniel as a kennel dog is not recommended. The isolation of a kennel environment will often irreparably harm the animal's personality, as it keeps him away from the people he so earnestly yearns to be with. Field Spaniels raised in kennel environments tend to exhibit a shyness that is difficult, if not impossible, to overcome.

LIVING WITH A FIELD SPANIEL

A highly developed sense of humor is characteristic of the Field Spaniel. In the endeavor to be part of every facet of the household, the Field Spaniel seems to understand when his human pack is entertained by his antics. A household full of guests is often the invitation for a Field Spaniel to entertain, whether this means retrieving dirty laundry to present to guests or carrying a tennis ball from guest to guest in search of a game of fetch.

Sharing a home with a Field Spaniel can be a challenge, but any annoyances are minor compared with the joy and companionship he will provide.

The drinking habits of the breed are legendary. Field Spaniels love water, whether to drink or play in, and the necessary accessibility of the water bowl allows the breed to combine both. It is not unusual for Field Spaniels to have a drink and bring some to their owners to share, dribbling rivulets of water en route. The long ears may become quite wet as the dogs drink and provide the perfect means for making wet trails around the house.

A long-time fancier once remarked that the notion of "house beautiful" is perhaps not an ideal to strive for when living with a Field Spaniel. In addition to their propensity for water, Field Spaniels do shed. While seasonal shedding of haircoat is predictably heavier as it heralds the arrival of spring, there is moderate shedding that occurs year-round.

When soundly asleep, many Field Spaniels snore, almost human-like in their slumbers. Some people will find this only a minor annoyance that is more than outweighed by the joy of owning a Field Spaniel. Other owners who are more apt to be kept awake by the snoring simply relegate the family pet to his own part of the house or a crate for sleeping during nighttime hours.

The diverse vocal range of the Field Spaniel is legendary, with an amazing range of vocalizations. From a deep-throated bark to a high-pitched squeal to

Field Spaniels are active dogs who need plenty of exercise and love to be outdoors. Choux-Choux and Toby can't wait to get out and play! Owners, Sue Strong and Sharon Douthit.

a distinctive yodel, the Field Spaniel readily expresses his preferences in a manner that is somehow human-like in his ability to communicate.

When awake, the Field Spaniel is ready for both work and games. If there is no outlet for this energetic drive, a Field Spaniel might seek to entertain himself. This may result in chewed furniture, incessant barking and other undesirable behaviors. Daily walks, obedience classes, games of "fetch" in a secure area, hunt training as well as agility and tracking pursuits are all excellent jobs for the Field Spaniel. These outlets serve to channel the Field Spaniel's intelli-

Field Spaniels tend to form close bonds with their owners and follow them wherever they go, even on vacation! The Evans's Field Spaniels accompanied them to Maine.

gence and energy and are equally as enjoyable for his owner.

Field Spaniels have a penchant for thievery, particularly of food items. More than one Field Spaniel owner tells the tale of the disappearance of a roast thawing for dinner from the kitchen counter. While their height does not allow the Field Spaniel to easily reach the top of a counter, the breed is innovative in determining methods of reaching a desired object or food item. In addition, a Field Spaniel will seek out objects that are handled frequently by their human owners. This is, in a way, a tribute to their fondness for their owners. However, owners often tell of the disappearance or occasional destruction of library books, remote controllers and other such frequently handled items that carry their smell.

Behaviors that are undesirable can develop quickly and become difficult to extinguish. For example, the breed is especially adept at using the expressive face and eyes to wheedle tidbits of food if allowed to beg during his owner's meal or snack times. While this is something that can be readily dealt with by training, the Field Spaniel with his fine intelligence will remember that, even on rare occasion, begging works. This means simply that owners must be careful to be consistent in dealing with behaviors that might be better not learned in the first place.

SPECIAL ABILITIES

The Field Spaniel is well suited to a variety of different pursuits. Competitive and leisure activities in which Field Spaniels excel include: hunting and tracking, where natural instincts may be refined with training; obedience, where the intelligence of the breed may be readily incorporated into training that emphasizes the teamwork of the dog and handler; and agility, where natural speed and maneuverability make the Field Spaniel a formidable competitor.

Field Spaniels also excel in pursuits that do not result in official titles or ribbons. They have been successfully trained as service dogs. In this role, the Field Spaniel, although too small to pull a wheelchair, is especially suited to the owner who requires assis-

Opposite: The Field Spaniel's trainability and retrieving instincts make them excellent assistance dogs. Casey is a full-time assistance dog for owner Mickey Burke.

Field Spaniels are highly intelligent dogs that can use their natural instincts to help others. This puppy is in training to become a therapy dog. Owner, Maxine Reed.

tance that makes use of the Field Spaniel's excellent retrieving abilities. Activities that range from picking up dropped objects, bringing a cordless telephone to their owner and alerting a hearing-impaired owner to the sound of a doorbell or alarm are ways in which Field Spaniels have been trained as service dogs.

Therapy work is another endeavor in which Field Spaniels excel, with the first accredited therapy dog Ch. Bitterblue's Charge Card, CD trained by owner Lynn G. Finney to visit extended care facilities in 1986. Since that time, many more Field Spaniels have achieved therapy dog accreditation and work in a variety of facilities with patients of a wide range of ages.

Law enforcement officers have also noticed the Field Spaniel, primarily for the superb scenting ability with which the breed is endowed in combination with the determined desire to succeed in any task the Field Spaniel is both trained for and commanded to perform. One representative of the breed has been trained to search and find firearms. Others have been trained for detection of illegal drugs. Although no Field Spaniels have yet been trained for search and rescue activities, it is probable that the breed would be equally as successful in this type of endeavor. The compact size of the Field Spaniel renders the breed as a viable alternative to other more well-known but much larger breeds used in law enforcement activities. The natural trainability, tractable nature, determination and medium size render the Field Spaniel ideally suited to a variety of serious tasks.

The Field Spaniel's versatility and adaptability make him "a dog for all seasons!" Ch. Calico's String Of Pearls owned by Sheila Miller.

GROOMING THE FIELD SPANIEL

Unlike many other spaniel breeds, the Field Spaniel carries a moderate coat. The coat is well-suited to the owner-handler who wants to show his dog, yet easy to maintain for the pet owner who is willing to spend but a few minutes a day grooming. Regular brushing and bathing along with an investment in basic grooming equipment will save countless dollars spent on visits to the grooming parlor. Only a minimal

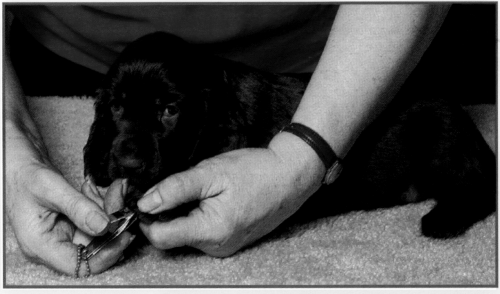

If you start grooming your Field Spaniel when he is a puppy, he will soon realize it can be a pleasurable experience and become used to the routine.

amount of trimming of the ears and feet is required for everyday wear. For show purposes, a bit more trimming on the head and throat will be necessary. The double coat sheds water easily, and while the feathers on the Field Spaniel's legs and ears may gather burrs during a day in the field, these can easily be removed with a bit of gentle grooming.

BASIC GROOMING EQUIPMENT NEEDS:
Bristle brush
Metal dog comb, medium/coarse style
Slicker brush
Flea comb

Thinning shears (blending shears)
Straight shears
Nail clipper
Styptic powder or solution
Cotton balls (large size preferred)
Ear cleaning solution
Dental care brush and toothpaste made for canines
Shampoo (for dark coats or all-purpose shampoo)
(Optional) All-purpose stripping knife (blade)
(Optional) Coat conditioner (for use after bathing)
(Optional) Daily coat conditioner spray with sunscreen additive
(Optional) Electric clipper with a #10F blade
(Optional) clipper blade #7F
(Optional) Small spray bottle with misting device; fill with distilled water
(Optional) Tackle box or other container to store grooming equipment

BASIC COAT CARE

Daily care includes a quick gentle, but thorough, brushing of the coat with a bristle-type brush. A metal dog comb may be used to remove any tangles from the feathering on the ears, legs, chest and belly. During times of the year when fleas are common, use a flea comb to check the coat thoroughly. Brush the coat with the lay of the coat, starting at the head and working gradually to the rear. Comb feathers gently, taking care to avoid pulling the feathering should a

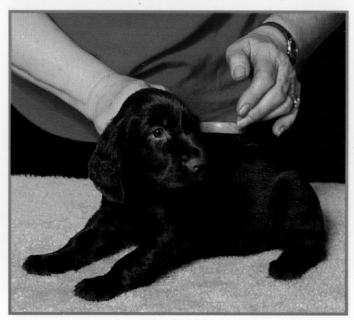

A regular grooming regimen is a great way to keep on top of any health or coat problems your Field Spaniel may have, as well as a way to spend quality time with your dog.

A metal dog comb can be used to remove any tangles from the feathering on the ears, chest, legs and belly. Owners, George and Dorothy O'Neil.

snarl be encountered. Misting the coat lightly with a spray bottle filled with distilled water avoids coat breakage during routine brushing and combing. If there is an old sturdy table available, placing a non-slip rug on top of the table and lifting the dog to the table top will make routine grooming chores easier to do. The rug will provide an adequate surface so that the dog does not slip. However, most routine grooming is easily completed while the dog lays on his owner's lap, perhaps while the owner is watching television. When done on a regular basis, most Field Spaniels truly enjoy this special time with their owner.

During times of heavier shedding, a slicker brush is helpful to remove dead coat. Use the slicker brush on the body coat only, never the feathering, as the slicker brush will tend to break and damage the feathered fringe on the ears, legs and underbelly. Using the metal comb or the flea comb may also be effective to remove dead coat and minimize shedding. Bathing a dog who is shedding will be helpful to loosen dead coat so that it may be removed. If bathed, the dog should be thoroughly dry prior to using the slicker brush.

TRIMMING

The Field Spaniel should have his head, ears, throat and feet trimmed monthly. This maintains the typical and classic look of the Field Spaniel head and trimming the feet allows the dog to benefit from the natural non-slip contact of the foot pad with the ground or floor. With blending shears, trim the face and muzzle. Whiskers on the muzzle may be left intact at the owner's discretion; although whiskers are generally removed for the show ring, this is not a requirement.

Prior to trimming the ears, place a cotton ball in the ear to prevent small hair particles from falling into and becoming embedded in the inner ear canal. The ears are generally trimmed with an electric clipper using a #10 blade to remove the hair from the top one-third of the ear on both the outer and inner side of the ear flap. However, this trimming may be accomplished through use of blending shears if an electric clipper is not available. Hair should also be removed from in front of the ear opening. Attention to trimming the ear increases the air circulation to the ear canal and is important in prevention of ear infections.

With the blending shear, blend the top of the ear, where the clipper line begins, to remove the sharp appearance of the clipper line. The top of the head is also blended to remove excess hair or curls; if an electric clipper is used, using a #7 blade while clipping with the natural lie of the hair is an alternative to decrease the amount of blending necessary to obtain a neat look to the head.

Use the blending shears to remove hair that grows out from between the toes of all four feet. The straight shear is used to remove hair from the bottom of the foot so that the hair is level with the pads as well as to neaten the outline of each foot. The trimmed foot should have a tidy and compact look.

If using an electric clipper at home, never be tempted to clip the body coat. Using electric clippers on the body coat often results in permanent damage to the texture of the haircoat. To neaten body coat, use a stripping knife to remove the excess.

BATHING

On an average of once a month, a Field Spaniel should be bathed. The need for bathing more or less will depend upon the amount of oil in the dog's coat as well as factors such as amount of time spent outdoors. The dog who is hunting in muddy or soggy terrain may require more frequent bathing. Any trimming that is required or ear cleaning should be completed prior to the bath.

Use a shampoo for dark coats or a general purpose shampoo formulated for dogs. Do not use a shampoo product formulated for human hair. Shampoo for canine use is specially formulated to maintain the

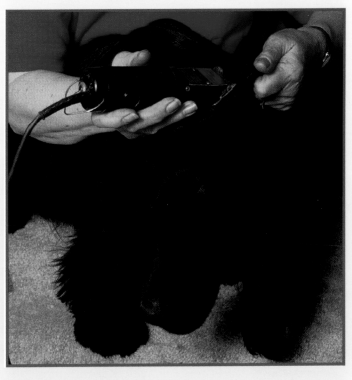

Attention to trimming the ear of the Field Spaniel increases the air circulation to the ear canal and is important in prevention of ear infections.

correct pH of the canine skin and haircoat. Many canine shampoos are also formulated to be non-irritating to the eyes.

A Field Spaniel may be easily bathed in the household bathtub. Avoid hair clogs in the tub drain by placing a length of nylon hosiery over the tub drain. This will trap hair loosened during bathing. Using tepid water, wet the dog's coat completely. Next, apply the shampoo as directed, taking care to avoid the face and eyes. Rinse the dog thoroughly, starting from the front and top and working while rinsing the shampoo toward the rear and back legs. A tub with a shower spray device on a hose is ideal for use in thorough rinsing. As an alternative, inexpensive tub faucet spray head/hose attachments are available for purchase. To complete the bath, use a soft damp washcloth to cleanse haircoat around the eyes and muzzle.

If desired, a coat conditioning rinse may be used, particularly on the feathering. Towel dry the dog; finish drying using a blow dryer set on no more than medium heat. While using the blow dryer, direct the air flow so that the coat is encouraged to lie flat while brushing in the natural direction of growth.

EAR CARE

Spaniels of any breed have a tendency to get ear infections due to the large and long ear that covers the ear canal. Routine ear cleaning on a weekly basis, in addition to monthly trimming the hair on the outer and inner ear, will go a long way toward preventing ear infections. Using a cotton ball, one for each ear, apply liquid ear cleaning solution. Wipe accumulated dirt and wax from all crevices in both ears.

NAILS

Although many dogs do not like to have their nails trimmed, it is a necessary procedure that keeps the feet in good shape. Long nails are thought to contribute to splaying of the toes, making it more likely that injury to the sensitive skin between the toes may occur. Using the nail clipper, cut the tips of each nail using a quick stroke while cutting to avoid pinching the nail. Avoid cutting into the quick or vein, although the dark nails of the Field Spaniel make it difficult, if not impossible, to see. If a nail bleeds, apply styptic powder or solution to the nail to stop the bleeding. If desired, rough nail edges following nail trimming may be smoothed with a metal nail file. Clipping the nails on a weekly basis, taking just the tips of the nails off each time, will keep nails short enough that the foot maintains proper shape.

TEN FAVORITE GROOMING TIPS OF FIELD SPANIEL FANCIERS

• A snood is helpful to keep long ears out of food during feeding times. This reduces the likelihood of tangling of ear feathering and goes a long way toward keeping the ears clean.

• An alternative to a snood is to purchase food and

Use your shears to remove the hair that grows out from between the toes of your dog's feet and check his paws for any cuts or tenderness.

water bowls that are specially shaped to be deeper and somewhat narrower than usual dog bowls. These are often called "spaniel bowls" and reduce the likelihood of ears dragging in food and water.

• For owners who prefer a more "natural" look, the outer ear may be stripped using a stripping blade, while the inner portion of the ear may be neatened by using thinning shears. The stripping blade may also be used to neaten hair on the throat and top of the head.

• An alternative to using a stripping blade or thinning shears to trim the hair around the ear canal is short blunt (ball-tipped) curved shears.

• Field Spaniels who work or play outdoors during the daytime may exhibit a progressive lightening of the haircoat as a result of the effects of the sun. The liver coat coloration is especially prone to sun-bleaching. Special conditioning coat sprays formulated with sunscreen are available to minimize sun damage to the haircoat.

- When trimming and bathing are required, clean the ears first. Use a cotton ball wet with the ear cleaning solution and squeezed to remove any excess fluid to protect the inner ear from small bits of hair during trimming and from bath water during bathing.
- Teaching a Field Spaniel to lay down on his side while feet are being trimmed makes the task of trimming feet much easier to perform.
- If using a canine shampoo that does not specify a "no tears" formulation, many fanciers recommend a single drop of pure mineral oil be instilled in each eye to prevent any irritation to the eyes as a result of shampoo.
- Disposable baby wipes are a good alternative for spot cleaning dirt from paws or for a quick daily cleaning of the outer ear canal.
- When there is a need to clean secretions that may collect at the inner corner of the eye, use a soft tissue, slightly dampened, and gently wipe moving from the inner corner of the eye to the outer corner. Use a separate tissue for each eye.

Nine-month-old Keeper (Ch. Woodrun's Yesterday) is looking his best, groomed and ready for the show ring. Owner, Karen Gracz.

BREED CONCERNS

In general, Field Spaniels are a healthy breed, with an average lifespan of 12 to 14 years. One of the founding dogs of the modern revival of the breed, Gormac Teal, reportedly lived to the ripe old age of 18 years. Providing for regular annual check-ups by a veterinarian are a basic responsibility of owning a Field Spaniel. In addition, routine home cleaning of a Field Spaniel's ears and teeth contributes to the overall health of the dog when combined with regular grooming.

EYES

Ectropion is probably the most common eye defect noted in the Field Spaniel. Simply defined, ectropion means "loose eyelids." More of a nuisance than a problem, the loose lower eyelid in and of itself is not very likely painful to the dog. It does, however, allow dust and other particulate matter to come in contact

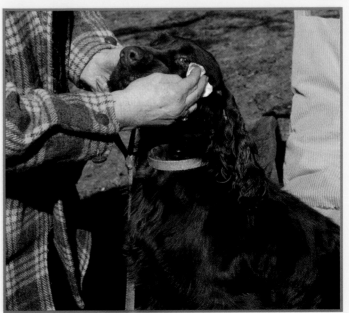

Field Spaniels are prone to a eye condition called ectropion that allows dirt and other irritants to come in contact with the eye. Make sure you keep your dog's eyes free of bacteria to prevent infections.

with the eye and cause irritation which will in turn result in excess tearing. The excess tearing provides a place for bacteria to grow so that if regular cleaning of the eyes is not provided, there will be a higher than normal potential for eye infection that could lead to more serious problems. If the ectropion is severe, it may be surgically corrected as recommended by a veterinarian.

Entropion is another defect of the outer lid structure of the eye that may be seen. Less common than ectropion, entropion is an inversion of the eyelid such that the lashes of the eyelid come into contact with the eye. Entropion is thought to have the potential for causing pain due to the continual irritation that occurs as the lashes brush the surface of the eye. Irritation and tearing will also be noted. Corrective surgery is likely to be required.

It is recommended that all Field Spaniels have a yearly eye examination by a veterinarian specially trained in canine ophthalmology. There are several eye defects known in Field Spaniels that may only be detected by the special examination techniques that allow visualization of the inner structures of the eyes. Eye defects that are seen occasionally are cataract, persistent pupillary membrane and multifocal retinal dysplasia. None of these have caused significant detrimental effects on the quality of life as based on reports of owners, though all have the potential to do so. The presence of inherited eye disorders will affect the decisions related to breeding the affected animal. Very uncommon but confirmed with the breed is progressive retinal atrophy (PRA), an eye disease marked by an initial impairment in night vision that progresses to daylight visual impairment and complete blindness. In general, PRA has a slow progression and may not be noted upon routine eye examination until a dog is four or more years of age. There is no treatment for PRA; affected animals should never be bred and the parents of such animals should be removed from any breeding program as well.

EARS

Routine ear cleaning is the best preventative measure against potential ear infection. Some Field Spaniels have a smaller than usual ear canal; these dogs will be more prone to ear infections and may require more frequent attention to keeping the ears clean and dry. Yeast infections of the ear are not uncommon.

This is largely due to the long heavy ear that covers the ear canal and thereby limits air flow. When combined with the Field Spaniel's penchant for water that results in wet feathering on the ears, the damp, warm and dark environment is ideal for yeast infections to occur. Yeast infections of the ear have a distinctive odor that is difficult to mistake for any other aroma. This type of infection can be difficult to eradicate and may tend to reoccur. Systematic attention to ear cleaning is the best prevention. Paying attention to the Field Spaniel's behavior to note any excessive shaking of the head or pawing at an ear in combination with observation of the ear during routine cleaning will alert the owner to the beginnings of a problem that may require veterinary intervention. Prompt veterinary intervention will help prevent further problems and reoccurrence.

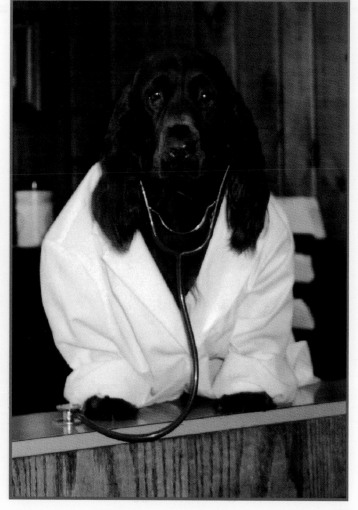

The doctor is in! Ch. Maplesugar Lady Emmaline knows that regular check-ups with her veterinarian are the key to maintaining good health. Owner, Eileen Griffin.

YOUR PUPPY'S NEW HOME

Before actually collecting your puppy, it is better that you purchase the basic items you will need in advance of the pup's arrival date. This allows you more opportunity to shop around and ensure you have exactly what you want rather than having to buy lesser quality in a hurry.

It is always better to collect the puppy as early in the day as possible. In most instances this will mean that the puppy has a few hours with your family before it is time to retire for his first night's sleep away from his former home.

If the breeder is local, then you may not need any form of box to place the puppy in when you bring him home. A member of the family can hold the pup in his lap—duly protected by some towels just in case the puppy becomes car sick! Be sure to advise the

Before you take your new puppy home, make sure that your family and your household are prepared for his arrival. Three-week-old pups owned by Becki Jo Wolkenheim.

Accustom your new Field Spaniel to his crate as soon as possible. Not only is it the safest way for him to travel but it also comes in handy at dog shows and the like.

breeder at what time you hope to arrive for the puppy, as this will obviously influence the feeding of the pup that morning or afternoon. If you arrive early in the day, then they will likely only give the pup a light breakfast so as to reduce the risk of travel sickness.

If the trip will be of a few hours duration, you should take a travel crate with you. The crate will provide your pup with a safe place to lie down and rest during the trip. During the trip, the puppy will no doubt wish to relieve his bowels, so you will have to make a few stops. On a long journey you may need a rest yourself, and can take the opportunity to let the puppy get some fresh air. However, do not let the puppy walk where there may have been a lot of other dogs because he might pick up an infection. Also, if he relieves his bowels at such a time, do not just leave the feces where they were dropped. This is the height of irre-sponsibility. It has resulted in many public parks and other places actually banning dogs. You can pur-chase poop-scoops from your pet shop and should have them with you whenever you are taking the dog out where he might foul a public place.

Your journey home should be made as quickly as possible. If it is a hot day, be sure the car interior is amply supplied with fresh air. It should never be too hot or too cold for the puppy. The pup must never be placed where he might be subject to a draft. If the journey requires an overnight stop at a motel, be

aware that other guests will not appreciate a puppy crying half the night. You must regard the puppy as a baby and comfort him so he does not cry for long periods. The worst thing you can do is to shout at or smack him. This will mean your relationship is off to a really bad start. You wouldn't smack a baby, and your puppy is still very much just this.

Who knows what surprises your puppy may have for you? It is best to be prepared for all situations in order to keep him safe and feeling secure.

ON ARRIVING HOME

By the time you arrive home the puppy may be very tired, in which case he should be taken to his sleeping area and allowed to rest. Children should not be allowed to interfere with the pup when he is sleeping. If the pup is not tired, he can be allowed to investigate his new home—but always under your close supervision. After a short look around, the puppy will no doubt appreciate a light meal and a drink of water. Do not overfeed him at his first meal because he will be in an excited state and more likely to be sick.

Although it is an obvious temptation, you should not invite friends and neighbors around to see the new arrival until he has had at least 48 hours in which to settle down. Indeed, if you can delay this longer then do so, especially if the puppy is not fully vaccinated. At the very least, the visitors might introduce some local bacteria on their clothing that the puppy is not immune to. This aspect is always a risk when a pup has been moved some distance, so the fewer people the pup meets in the first week or so the better.

DANGERS IN THE HOME

Your home holds many potential dangers for a little mischievous puppy, so you must think about these in advance and be sure he is protected from them. The more obvious are as follows:

Open Fires. All open fires should be protected by a mesh screen guard so there is no danger of the pup being burned by spitting pieces of coal or wood.

Electrical Wires. Puppies just love chewing on things, so be sure that all electrical appliances are neatly hidden from view and are not left plugged in when not in use. It is not sufficient simply to turn the plug switch to the off position—pull the plug from the socket.

Open Doors. A door would seem a pretty innocuous object, yet with a strong draft it could kill or injure a puppy easily if it is slammed shut. Always ensure there is no risk of this happening. It is most likely during warm weather when you have windows or outside doors open and a sudden gust of wind blows through.

Balconies. If you live in a high-rise building, obviously the pup must be protected from falling. Be sure he cannot get through any railings on your patio, balcony, or deck.

Ponds and Pools. A garden pond or a swimming pool is a very dangerous place for a little puppy to be near. Be sure it is well screened so there is no risk of

Children and puppies can become great pals, as long as the child is educated on the proper way to handle dogs. Tucker, owned by Nelson and Susan Bartlett, and friend.

the pup falling in. It takes barely a minute for a pup—
or a child—to drown.

The Kitchen. While many puppies will be kept in the
kitchen, at least while they are toddlers and not able
to control their bowel movements, this is a room full of
danger—especially while you are cooking. When
cooking, keep the puppy in a play pen or in another
room where he is safely out of harm's way. Alterna-
tively, if you have a carry box or crate, put him in this
so he can still see you but is well protected.

Be aware, when using washing machines, that
more than one puppy has clambered in and decided
to have a nap and received a wash instead! If you
leave the washing machine door open and leave the
room for any reason, then be sure to check inside the
machine before you close the door and switch on.

Small Children. Toddlers and small children should
never be left unsupervised with puppies. In spite of
such advice it is amazing just how many people not
only do this but also allow children to pull and maul
pups. They should be taught from the outset that a
puppy is not a plaything to be dragged about the
home—and they should be promptly scolded if they
disobey.

Children must be shown how to lift a puppy so it is
safe. Failure by you to correctly educate your children
about dogs could one day result in their getting a very
nasty bite or scratch. When a puppy is lifted, his
weight must always be supported. To lift the pup, first
place your right hand under his chest. Next, secure
the pup by using your left hand to hold his neck. Now
you can lift him and bring him close to your chest.
Never lift a pup by his ears and, while he can be lifted
by the scruff of his neck where the fur is loose, there
is no reason ever to do this, so don't.

Beyond the dangers already cited you may be able
to think of other ones that are specific to your home—
steep basement steps or the like. Go around your
home and check out all potential problems—you'll be
glad you did.

THE FIRST NIGHT

The first few nights a puppy spends away from his
mother and littermates are quite traumatic for him. He
will feel very lonely, maybe cold, and will certainly
miss the heartbeat of his siblings when sleeping. To
help overcome his loneliness it may help to place a
clock next to his bed—one with a loud tick. This will in

some way soothe him, as the clock ticks to a rhythm not dissimilar from a heart beat. A cuddly toy may also help in the first few weeks. A dim nightlight may provide some comfort to the puppy, because his eyes will not yet be fully able to see in the dark. The puppy may want to leave his bed for a drink or to relieve himself.

If the pup does whimper in the night, there are two things you should not do. One is to get up and chastise him, because he will not understand why you are shouting at him; and the other is to rush to comfort him every time he cries because he will quickly realize that if he wants you to come running all he needs to do is to holler loud enough!

By all means give your puppy some extra attention

When it is time for a puppy to go to his new home, he will miss the company of his littermates. Owners, George and Dorothy O'Neil.

on his first night, but after this quickly refrain from so doing. The pup will cry for a while but then settle down and go to sleep. Some pups are, of course, worse than others in this respect, so you must use balanced judgment in the matter. Many owners take their pups to bed with them, and there is certainly nothing wrong with this.

The pup will be no trouble in such cases. However, you should only do this if you intend to let this be a permanent arrangement, otherwise it is hardly fair to the puppy. If you have decided to have two puppies, then they will keep each other company and you will have few problems.

OTHER PETS

If you have other pets in the home then the puppy

must be introduced to them under careful supervision. Puppies will get on just fine with any other pets—but you must make due allowance for the respective sizes of the pets concerned, and appreciate that your puppy has a rather playful nature. It would be very foolish to leave him with a young rabbit. The pup will want to play and might bite the bunny and get altogether too rough with it. Kittens are more able to defend themselves from overly cheeky pups, who will get a quick scratch if they overstep the mark. The adult cat could obviously give the pup a very bad scratch, though generally cats will jump clear of pups

Your Field Spaniel puppies will keep busy if they have Nylabones® to chew on. They are made of non-toxic durable polyurethane and help break up plaque on your dog's teeth.

Field Spaniels get along well with other members of their breed as well as other pets. Owners, George and Dorothy O'Neil.

and watch them from a suitable vantage point. Eventually they will meet at ground level where the cat will quickly hiss and box a puppy's ears. The pup will soon learn to respect an adult cat; thereafter they will probably develop into great friends as the pup matures into an adult dog.

HOUSETRAINING

Undoubtedly, the first form of training your puppy will undergo is in respect of his toilet habits. To achieve this you can use either newspaper, or a large litter tray filled with soil or lined with newspaper. A puppy cannot control his bowels until he is a few months old, and not fully until he is an adult. Therefore you must anticipate his needs and be prepared for a few accidents. The prime times a pup will urinate and defecate are shortly after he wakes up from a sleep, shortly after he has eaten, and after he has been playing awhile. He will usually whimper and start searching the room for a suitable place. You must quickly pick him up and place him on the newspaper or in the litter tray. Hold him in position gently but firmly. He might jump out of the box without doing anything on the first one or two occasions, but if you simply repeat the procedure every time you think he wants to relieve himself then eventually he will get the message.

When he does defecate as required, give him plenty of praise, telling him what a good puppy he is. The litter tray or newspaper must, of course, be cleaned or replaced after each use—puppies do not like using a dirty toilet any more than you do. The pup's toilet can be placed near the kitchen door and as he gets older the tray can be placed outside while the door is open. The pup will then start to use it while he is outside. From that time on, it is easy to get the pup to use a given area of the yard.

Many breeders recommend the popular alternative of crate training. Upon bringing the pup home, introduce him to his crate. The open wire crate is the best choice, placed in a restricted, draft-free area of the home. Put the pup's Nylabone® and other favorite toys in the crate along with a wool blanket or other suitable bedding. The puppy's natural cleanliness instincts prohibit him from soiling in the place where he sleeps, his crate. The puppy should be allowed to go in and out of the open crate during the day, but he should sleep in the crate at night and at intervals during the day. Whenever the pup is taken out of his crate, he should be brought outside (or to his newspapers) to do his business. Never use the crate as a place of punishment. You will see how quickly your pup takes to his crate, considering it as his own safe haven from the big world around him.

THE EARLY DAYS

You will no doubt be given much advice on how to bring up your puppy. This will come from dog-owning friends, neighbors, and through articles and books you may read on the subject. Some of the advice will be sound, some will be nothing short of rubbish. What you should do above all else is to keep an open mind and let common sense prevail over prejudice and worn-out ideas that have been handed down over the centuries. There is no one way that is superior to all others, no more than there is no one dog that is exactly a replica of another. Each is an individual and must always be regarded as such.

A dog never becomes disobedient, unruly, or a menace to society without the full consent of his owner. Your puppy may have many limitations, but the singular biggest limitation he is confronted with in so many instances is his owner's inability to understand his needs and how to cope with them.

IDENTIFICATION

It is a sad reflection on our society that the number of dogs and cats stolen every year runs into many thousands. To these can be added the number that get lost. If you do not want your cherished pet to be lost or stolen, then you should see that he is carrying a permanent identification number, as well as a temporary tag on his collar.

Permanent markings come in the form of tattoos placed either inside the pup's ear flap, or on the inner side of a pup's upper rear leg. The number given is then recorded with one of the national registration companies. Research laboratories will not purchase dogs carrying numbers as they realize these are clearly someone's pet, and not abandoned animals. As a result, thieves will normally abandon dogs so marked and this at least gives the dog a chance to be

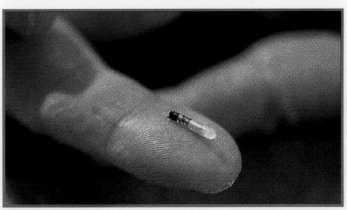

The newest method of identification is the microchip, a computer chip that is no bigger than a grain of rice, that is injected into the dog's skin.

taken to the police or the dog pound, when the number can be traced and the dog reunited with its family. The only problem with this method at this time is that there are a number of registration bodies, so it is not always apparent which one the dog is registered with (as you provide the actual number). However, each registration body is aware of his competitors and will normally be happy to supply their addresses. Those holding the dog can check out which one you are with. It is not a perfect system, but until such is developed it's the best available.

A temporary tag takes the form of a metal or plastic disk large enough for you to place the dog's name and your phone number on it—maybe even your address as well. In virtually all places you will be required to obtain a license for your puppy. This may not become applicable until the pup is six months old, but it might apply regardless of his age. Much depends upon the state within a country, or the country itself, so check with your veterinarian if the breeder has not already advised you on this.

FEEDING YOUR FIELD SPANIEL

Dog owners today are fortunate in that they live in an age when considerable cash has been invested in the study of canine nutritional requirements. This means dog food manufacturers are very concerned about ensuring that their foods are of the best quality. The result of all of their studies, apart from the food itself, is that dog owners are bombarded with advertisements telling them why they must purchase a

given brand. The number of products available to you is unlimited, so it is hardly surprising to find that dogs in general suffer from obesity and an excess of vitamins, rather than the reverse. Be sure to feed age-appropriate food—puppy food up to one year of age, adult food thereafter. Generally, breeders recommend dry food supplemented by canned, if needed.

Newborn puppies get their first nutrients from their mother, but as they get older it becomes the owner's responsibility to provide his pup with balanced meals.

FACTORS AFFECTING NUTRITIONAL NEEDS

Activity Level. A dog that lives in a country environment and is able to exercise for long periods of the day will need more food than the same breed of dog living in an apartment and given little exercise.

Quality of the Food. Obviously the quality of food will affect the quantity required by a puppy. If the nutritional content of a food is low then the puppy will need more of it than if a better quality food was fed.

Balance of Nutrients and Vitamins. Feeding a puppy the correct balance of nutrients is not easy because the average person is not able to measure out ratios of one to another, so it is a case of trying to see that nothing is in excess. However, only tests, or your veterinarian, can be the source of reliable advice.

Genetic and Biological Variation. Apart from all of the other considerations, it should be remembered that each puppy is an individual. His genetic make-up will influence not only its physical characteristics but also his metabolic efficiency. This being so, two pups from the same litter can vary quite a bit in the amount of food they need to perform the same function under

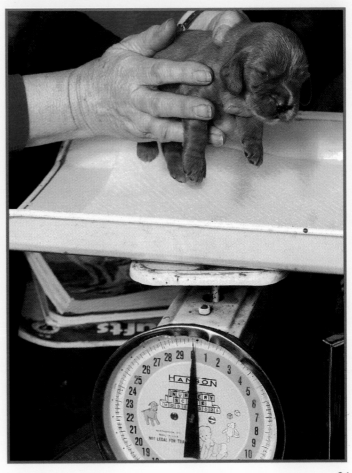

From the very beginning, proper nutrition is essential for the growth and development of the dog.

the same conditions. If you consider the potential combinations of all of these factors then you will see that pups of a given breed could vary quite a bit in the amount of food they will need. Before discussing feeding quantities it is valuable to know at least a little about the composition of food and its role in the body.

COMPOSITION AND ROLE OF FOOD

The main ingredients of food are protein, fats, and carbohydrates, each of which is needed in relatively large quantities when compared to the other needs of vitamins and minerals. The other vital ingredient of food is, of course, water. Although all foods obviously contain some of the basic ingredients needed for an animal to survive, they do not all contain the ingredients in the needed ratios or type. For example, there are many forms of protein, just as there are many types of carbohydrates. Both of these compounds are found in meat and in vegetable matter—but not all of those that are needed will be in one particular meat or vegetable. Plants, especially, do not contain certain amino acids that are required for the synthesis of certain proteins needed by dogs.

Likewise, vitamins are found in meats and vegetable matter, but vegetables are a richer source of most. Meat contains very little carbohydrates. Some vitamins can be synthesized by the dog, so do not need to be supplied via the food. Dogs are carnivores and this means their digestive tract has evolved to need a high quantity of meat as compared to humans. The digestive system of carnivores is unable to break down the tough cellulose walls of plant matter, but it is easily able to assimilate proteins from meat.

In order to gain its needed vegetable matter in a form that it can cope with, the carnivore eats all of its prey. This includes the partly digested food within the

Carrots are rich in fiber, carbohydrates, and vitamin A. The CarrotBone™ by Nylabone® is a durable chew containing no plastics or artificial ingredients and it can be served as-is, in a bone-hard form, or microwaved to a biscuity consistency.

stomach. In commercially prepared foods, the cellulose is broken down by cooking. During this process the vitamin content is either greatly reduced or lost altogether. The manufacturer therefore adds vitamins once the heat process has been completed. This is why commercial foods are so useful as part of a feeding regimen, providing they are of good quality and from a company that has prepared the foods very carefully.

Proteins

These are made from amino acids, of which at least ten are essential if a puppy is to maintain healthy growth. Proteins provide the building blocks for the puppy's body. The richest sources are meat, fish and

A good-quality dog food is necessary to maintain your dog's high energy level and basic good health.

poultry, together with their by-products. The latter will include milk, cheese, yogurt, fishmeal, and eggs. Vegetable matter that has a high protein content includes soy beans, together with numerous corn and other plant extracts that have been dehydrated. The actual protein content needed in the diet will be determined both by the activity level of the dog and his age. The total protein need will also be influenced by the digestibility factor of the food given.

Fats

These serve numerous roles in the puppy's body. They provide insulation against the cold, and help buffer the organs from knocks and general activity

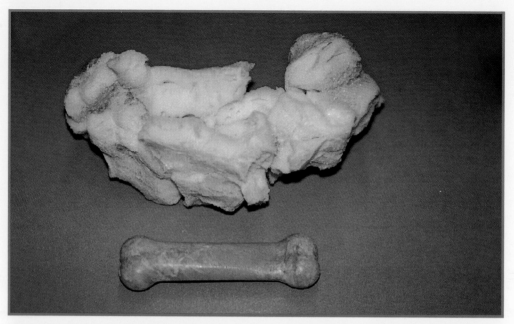

shocks. They provide the richest source of energy, and reserves of this, and they are vital in the transport of vitamins and other nutrients, via the blood, to all other organs. Finally, it is the fat content within a diet that gives it palatability. It is important that the fat content of a diet should not be excessive. This is because the high energy content of fats (more than twice that of protein or carbohydrate) will increase the overall energy content of the diet. The puppy will adjust its food intake to that of its energy needs, which are obviously more easily met in a high-energy diet. This will mean that while the fats are providing the energy needs of the puppy, the overall diet may not be providing its protein, vitamin, and mineral needs, so signs of protein deficiency will become apparent. Rich sources of fats are meat, their byproducts (butter, milk), and vegetable oils, such as safflower, olive, corn or soy bean.

POPpups™ are 100% edible and enhanced with dog friendly ingredients like liver, cheese, spinach, carrots or potatoes. They contain no salt, sugar, alcohol, plastic, or preservatives. You can even microwave a POPpup™ to turn into a huge crackly treat.

Carbohydrates

These are the principal energy compounds given to puppies and adult dogs. Their inclusion within most commercial brand dog foods is for cost, rather than dietary needs. These compounds are more commonly known as sugars, and they are seen in simple or complex compounds of carbon, hydrogen, and oxygen. One of the simple sugars is called glucose, and it is vital to many metabolic processes. When large chains of glucose are created, they form compound sugars. One of these is called glycogen, and it is found in the cells of animals. Another, called starch, is the material that is found in the cells of plants.

Vitamins

These are not foods as such but chemical compounds that assist in all aspects of an animal's life. They help in so many ways that to attempt to describe these effectively would require a chapter in itself. Fruits are a rich source of vitamins, as is the liver of most animals. Many vitamins are unstable and easily destroyed by light, heat, moisture, or rancidity. An excess of vitamins, especially A and D, has been proven to be very harmful. Provided a puppy is receiving a balanced diet, it is most unlikely there will be a deficiency, whereas hypervitaminosis (an excess of vitamins) has become quite common due to owners and breeders feeding unneeded supplements. The only time you should feed extra vitamins to your puppy is if your veterinarian advises you to.

Minerals

These provide strength to bone and cell tissue, as well as assist in many metabolic processes. Examples are calcium, phosphorous, copper, iron, magnesium, selenium, potassium, zinc, and sodium. The recommended amounts of all minerals in the diet has not been fully established. Calcium and phosphorous are known to be important, especially to puppies. They help in forming strong bone. As with vitamins, a

Roar-Hide® is completely edible and is high in protein (over 86%) and low in fat (less than one-third of 1%). Unlike common rawhide, it is safer, less messy, and more fun.

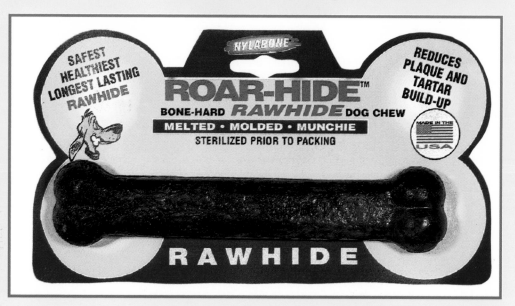

If you keep your dogs on a regular feeding schedule, they will expect their meals at the same time every day.

mineral deficiency is most unlikely in pups given a good and varied diet. Again, an excess can create problems—this applying equally to calcium.

Water

This is the most important of all nutrients, as is easily shown by the fact that the adult dog is made up of about 60 percent water, the puppy containing an even higher percentage. Dogs must retain a water balance, which means that the total intake should be balanced by the total output. The intake comes either by direct input (the tap or its equivalent), plus water released when food is oxidized, known as metabolic water (remember that all foods contain the elements hydrogen and oxygen that recombine in the body to create water). A dog without adequate water will lose condition more rapidly than one depleted of food, a fact common to most animal species.

AMOUNT TO FEED

The best way to determine dietary requirements is by observing the puppy's general health and physical appearance. If he is well covered with flesh, shows good bone development and muscle, and is an active alert puppy, then his diet is fine. A puppy will consume about twice as much as an adult (of the same breed). You should ask the breeder of your puppy to show you the amounts fed to their pups and this will be a good starting point.

The puppy should eat his meal in about five to seven minutes. Any leftover food can be discarded or placed into the refrigerator until the next meal (but be sure it is thawed fully if your fridge is very cold).

If the puppy quickly devours its meal and is clearly still hungry, then you are not giving him enough food. If he eats readily but then begins to pick at it, or walks away leaving a quantity, then you are probably giving him too much food. Adjust this at the next meal and you will quickly begin to appreciate what the correct amount is. If, over a number of weeks, the pup starts to look fat, then he is obviously overeating; the reverse is true if he starts to look thin compared with others of the same breed.

Your Field Spaniel's balanced diet will be evident in his shiny coat and overall appearance. Ch. Tamoshire Midnight Rendezvous owned by Susan Strong and Sharon Douthit.

WHEN TO FEED

It really does not matter what times of the day the puppy is fed, as long as he receives the needed quantity of food. Puppies from 8 weeks to 12 or 16 weeks need 3 or 4 meals a day. Older puppies and adult dogs should be fed twice a day. What is most important is that the feeding times are reasonably regular. They can be tailored to fit in with your own timetable—for example, 7 a.m. and 6 p.m. The dog will then expect his meals at these times each day. Keeping regular feeding times and feeding set amounts will help you monitor your puppy's or dog's health. If a dog that's normally enthusiastic about mealtimes and eats readily suddenly shows a lack of interest in food, you'll know something's not right.

The amount of food you feed your dog will depend on his energy level and his age. J. Ralph Alderfer and his seven Field Spaniels enjoying a snack. Looks like they can't wait!

TRAINING YOUR FIELD SPANIEL

Once your puppy has settled into your home and responds to his name, then you can begin his basic training. Before giving advice on how you should go about doing this, two important points should be made. You should train the puppy in isolation of any potential distractions, and you should keep all lessons very short. It is essential that you have the full attention of your puppy. This is not possible if there are other people about, or televisions and radios on,

Field Spaniels excel in activities that make the most of their superb nose. Maplesugar Carrilon working a track. Owner, D. Kay Klein.

or other pets in the vicinity. Even when the pup has become a young adult, the maximum time you should allocate to a lesson is about 20 minutes. However, you can give the puppy more than one lesson a day, three being as many as are recommended, each well spaced apart.

Before beginning a lesson, always play a little game with the puppy so he is in an active state of mind and thus more receptive to the matter at hand. Likewise, always end a lesson with fun-time for the pup, and always—this is most important—end on a high

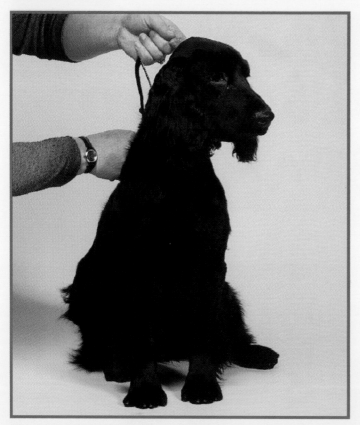

Your dog should become accustomed to his collar and leash before you begin training exercises.

note, praising the puppy. Let the lesson end when the pup has done as you require so he receives lots of fuss. This will really build his confidence.

COLLAR AND LEASH TRAINING

Training a puppy to his collar and leash is very easy. Place a collar on the puppy and, although he will initially try to bite at it, he will soon forget it, the more so if you play with him. You can leave the collar on for a few hours. Some people leave their dogs' collars on all of the time, others only when they are taking the dog out. If it is to be left on, purchase a narrow or round one so it does not mark the fur.

Once the puppy ignores his collar, then you can attach the leash to it and let the puppy pull this along behind it for a few minutes. However, if the pup starts to chew at the leash, simply hold the leash but keep it slack and let the pup go where he wants. The idea is to let him get the feel of the leash, but not get in the habit of chewing it. Repeat this a couple of times a day for two days and the pup will get used to the leash without thinking that it will restrain him—which you will not have attempted to do yet.

Next, you can let the pup understand that the leash will restrict his movements. The first time he realizes this, he will pull and buck or just sit down. Immediately call the pup to you and give him lots of fuss. Never tug on the leash so the puppy is dragged along the floor, as this simply implants a negative thought in his mind.

COME

Come is the most vital of all commands and especially so for the independently minded dog. To teach the puppy to come, let him reach the end of a long lead, then give the command and his name, gently pulling him toward you at the same time. As soon as he associates the word come with the action of moving toward you, pull only when he does not respond immediately. As he starts to come, move

Nigel, the first Field Spaniel to earn an agility title, shows his prowess at the agility open tunnel. Owner, Eric Hendrikson.

back to make him learn that he must come from a distance as well as when he is close to you. Soon you may be able to practice without a leash, but if he is slow to come or notably disobedient, go to him and pull him toward you, repeating the command. Never scold a dog during this exercise—or any other exercise. Remember the trick is that the puppy must want to come to you. For the very independent dog, hand signals may work better than verbal commands.

THE SIT COMMAND

As with most basic commands, your puppy will learn this one in just a few lessons. You can give the puppy two lessons a day on the sit command but he will make just as much progress with one 15-minute lesson each day. Some trainers will advise you that you should not proceed to other commands until the previous one has been learned really well. However, a bright young pup is quite capable of handling more than one command per lesson, and certainly per day. Indeed, as time progresses, you will be going through each command as a matter of routine before a new one is attempted. This is so the puppy always starts, as well as ends, a lesson on a high note, having successfully completed something.

Call the puppy to you and fuss over him. Place one hand on his hindquarters and the other under his upper chest. Say "Sit" in a pleasant (never harsh) voice. At the same time, push down his rear end and push up under his chest. Now lavish praise on the puppy. Repeat this a few times and your pet will get the idea. Once the puppy is in the sit position you will release your hands. At first he will tend to get up, so immediately repeat the exercise. The lesson will end when the pup is in the sit position. When the puppy understands the command, and does it right away, you can slowly move backwards so that you are a few feet away from him. If he attempts to come to you, simply place him back in the original position and start again. Do not attempt to keep the pup in the sit position for too long. At this age, even a few seconds is a long while and you do not want him to get bored with lessons before he has even begun them.

THE HEEL COMMAND

All dogs should be able to walk nicely on a leash without their owners being involved in a tug-of-war. The heel command will follow leash training. Heel training is best done where you have a wall to one side of you. This will restrict the puppy's lateral movements, so you only have to contend with forward and backward situations. A fence is an alternative, or you can do the lesson in the garage. Again, it is better to do the lesson in private, not on a public sidewalk where there will be many distractions.

With a puppy, there will be no need to use a choke collar as you can be just as effective with a regular one. The leash should be of good length, certainly not too short. You can adjust the space between you, the puppy, and the wall so your pet has only a small amount of room to move sideways. This being so, he will either hang back or pull ahead—the latter is the more desirable state as it indicates a bold pup who is not frightened of you.

The Field Spaniel's ability to learn quickly and his desire to please his owner make him a natural in obedience competition. Ch. Calico's Baird, CD heels for owner Cheryl Benedict.

Hold the leash in your right hand and pass it through your left. As the puppy moves ahead and strains on the leash, give the leash a quick jerk backwards with your left hand, at the same time saying "Heel." The position you want the pup to be in is such that his chest is level with, or just behind, an imaginary line from your knee. When the puppy is in this position, praise him and begin walking again, and the whole exercise will be repeated. Once the puppy begins to get the message, you can use your left hand to pat the side of your knee so the pup is encouraged to keep close to your side.

It is useful to suddenly do an about-turn when the pup understands the basics. The puppy will now be behind you, so you can pat your knee and say "Heel." As soon as the pup is in the correct position, give him lots of praise. The puppy will now be beginning to associate certain words with certain actions. Whenever he is not in the heel position he will experience displeasure as you jerk the leash, but when he comes alongside you he will receive praise. Given these two options, he will always prefer the latter—assuming he has no other reason to fear you, which would then create a dilemma in his mind.

Once the lesson has been well learned, then you can adjust your pace from a slow walk to a quick one and the puppy will come to adjust. The slow walk is always the more difficult for most puppies, as they are usually anxious to be on the move.

If you have no wall to walk against then things will be a little more difficult because the pup will tend to wander to his left. This means you need to give lateral jerks as well as bring the pup to your side. End the lesson when the pup is walking nicely beside you. Begin the lesson with a few sit commands (which he understands by now), so you're starting with success and praise. If your puppy is nervous on the leash, you should never drag him to your side as you may see so many other people do (who obviously didn't invest in a good book like you did!). If the pup sits down, call him to your side and give lots of praise. The pup must always come to you because he wants to. If he is dragged to your side he will see you doing the dragging—a big negative. When he races ahead he does not see you jerk the leash, so all he knows is that something restricted his movement and, once he was in a given position, you gave him lots of praise. This is using canine psychology to your advantage.

Always try to remember that if a dog must be disciplined, then try not to let him associate the discipline with you. This is not possible in all matters but, where it is, this is definitely to be preferred.

THE STAY COMMAND

This command follows from the sit. Face the puppy

Puppies have a short attention span. Make sure to keep training lessons short so that your Field Spaniel pup doesn't lose interest.

and say "Sit." Now step backwards, and as you do, say "Stay." Let the pup remain in the position for only a few seconds before calling him to you and giving lots of praise. Repeat this, but step further back. You do not need to shout at the puppy. Your pet is not deaf; in fact, his hearing is far better than yours. Speak just loudly enough for the pup to hear, yet use a firm voice. You can stretch the word to form a "sta-a-a-y." If the pup gets up and comes to you simply lift him up, place him back in the original position, and start again. As the pup comes to understand the command, you can move further and further back.

Field Spaniels have an instinctual love of the water that makes them natural hunters and retrievers. Owner, Sarah W. Evans.

The next test is to walk away after placing the pup. This will mean your back is to him, which will tempt him

to follow you. Keep an eye over your shoulder, and the minute the pup starts to move, spin around and, using a sterner voice, say either "Sit" or "Stay." If the pup has gotten quite close to you, then, again, return him to the original position.

As the weeks go by you can increase the length of time the pup is left in the stay position—but two to three minutes is quite long enough for a puppy. If your puppy drops into a lying position and is clearly more comfortable, there is nothing wrong with this. Likewise, your pup will want to face the direction in which you walked off. Some trainers will insist that the dog faces the direction he was placed in, regardless of whether you move off on his blind side. I have never believed in this sort of obedience because it has no practical benefit.

THE DOWN COMMAND

From the puppy's viewpoint, the down command can

be one of the more difficult ones to accept. This is because the position is one taken up by a submissive dog in a wild pack situation. A timid dog will roll over—a natural gesture of submission. A bolder pup will want to get up, and might back off, not feeling he should have to submit to this command. He will feel that he is under attack from you and about to be punished—which is what would be the position in his natural environment. Once he comes to understand this is not the case, he will accept this unnatural position without any problem.

You may notice that some dogs will sit very quickly, but will respond to the down command more slowly—it is their way of saying that they will obey the command, but under protest!

There two ways to teach this command. One is, in my mind, more intimidating than the other, but it is up to you to decide which one works best for you. The first method is to stand in front of your puppy and bring him to the sit position, with his collar and leash on. Pass the leash under your left foot so that when you pull on it, the result is that the pup's neck is forced downwards. With your free left hand, push the pup's shoulders down while at the same time saying "Down." This is when a bold pup will instantly try to back off and wriggle in full protest. Hold the pup firmly by the shoulders so he stays in the position for a second or two, then tell him what a good dog he is and give him lots of praise. Repeat this only a few times in a lesson because otherwise the puppy will get bored and upset over this command. End with an easy command that brings back the pup's confidence.

The second method, and the one I prefer, is done as follows: Stand in front of the pup and then tell him to sit. Now kneel down, which is immediately far less intimidating to the puppy than to have you towering above him. Take each of his front legs and pull them forward, at the same time saying "Down." Release the legs and quickly apply light pressure on the shoulders with your left hand. Then, as quickly, say "Good boy" and give lots of fuss. Repeat two or three times only. The pup will learn over a few lessons. Remember, this is a very submissive act on the pup's behalf, so there is no need to rush matters.

RECALL TO HEEL COMMAND

When your puppy is coming to the heel position from an off-leash situation—such as if he has been running free—he should do this in the correct manner. He should pass behind you and take up his position and then sit. To teach this command, have the pup in front of you in the sit position with his collar and leash on. Hold the leash in your right hand. Give him the command to heel, and pat your left knee. As the pup starts to move forward, use your right hand to guide him behind you. If need be you can hold his collar and walk the dog around the back of you to the desired position. You will need to repeat this a few times until the dog understands what is wanted.

When he has done this a number of times, you can try it without the collar and leash. If the pup comes up toward your left side, then bring him to the sit position in front of you, hold his collar and walk him around the back of you. He will eventually understand and automatically pass around your back each time. If the dog is already behind you when you recall him, then he should automatically come to your left side, which you will be patting with your hand.

The Field Spaniel is a dog of many talents and can be taught to excel at all types of competitions. Owner, Eric Hendrikson.

THE NO COMMAND

This is a command that must be obeyed every time without fail. There are no halfway stages, he must be 100-percent reliable. Most delinquent dogs have never been taught this command; included in these are the jumpers, the barkers, and the biters. Were your puppy to approach a poisonous snake or any other potential danger, the no command, coupled with the recall, could save his life. You do not need to give a specific lesson for this command because it will crop up time and again in day-to-day life.

If the puppy is chewing a slipper, you should approach the pup, take hold of the slipper, and say "No" in a stern voice. If he jumps onto the furniture, lift him off and say "No" and place him gently on the floor. You must be consistent in the use of the command and apply it every time he is doing something you do not want him to do.

YOUR HEALTHY FIELD SPANIEL

Dogs, like all other animals, are capable of contracting problems and diseases that, in most cases, are easily avoided by sound husbandry—meaning well-bred and well-cared-for animals are less prone to developing diseases and problems than are carelessly bred and neglected animals. Your knowledge of how to avoid problems is far more valuable than all of the books and advice on how to cure them. Respectively, the only person you should listen to about treatment is your vet. Veterinarians don't have all the answers, but at least they are trained to analyze and treat illnesses, and are aware of the full implications of treatments. This does not mean a few old remedies aren't good standbys when all else fails, but in most cases modern science provides the best treatments for disease.

Opposite: Veterinarians are trained to analyze and treat illnesses. Having complete trust in your chosen veterinarian is tantamount to the long life of your dog.

PHYSICAL EXAMS

Your puppy should receive regular physical examinations or check-ups. These come in two forms. One is obviously performed by your vet, and the other is a day-to-day procedure that should be done by you. Apart from the fact the exam will highlight any problem at an early stage, it is an excellent way of socializing the pup to being handled.

To do the physical exam yourself, start at the head and work your way around the body. You are looking for any sign of lesions, or any indication of parasites on the pup. The most common parasites are fleas and ticks.

A thorough oral exam should be a part of your Field Spaniel's regular check-up.

HEALTHY TEETH AND GUMS

Chewing is instinctual. Puppies chew so that their teeth and jaws grow strong and healthy as they develop. As the permanent teeth begin to emerge, it is painful and annoying to the puppy, and puppy owners must recognize that their new charges need something safe upon which to chew. Unfortunately, once the puppy's permanent teeth have emerged and settled solidly into the jaw, the chewing instinct does not fade. Adult dogs instinctively need to clean their teeth, massage their gums, and exercise their jaws through chewing.

It is necessary for your dog to have clean teeth. You should take your dog to the veterinarian at least once a year to have his teeth cleaned and to have his mouth examined for any sign of oral disease. Although dogs do not get cavities in the same way humans do, dogs' teeth accumulate tartar, and more quickly than hu-

The Hercules® has raised dental tips that help fight plaque on your Field Spaniel's teeth and gums.

mans do! Veterinarians recommend brushing your dog's teeth daily. But who can find time to brush their dog's teeth daily? The accumulation of tartar and plaque on our dog's teeth when not removed can cause irritation and eventually erode the enamel and finally destroy the teeth. Advanced cases, while destroying the teeth, bring on gingivitis and periodontitis, two very serious conditions that can affect the dog's internal organs as well...to say nothing about bad breath!

Since everyone can't brush their dog's teeth daily or get to the veterinarian often enough for him to scale

Nylafloss® does wonders for your Field Spaniel's dental health by massaging his gums and literally flossing between his teeth, loosening plaque and tartar build-up. Unlike cotton tug toys, Nylafloss® won't rot or fray.

the dog's teeth, providing the dog with something safe to chew on will help maintain oral hygeine. Chew devices from Nylabone® keep dogs' teeth clean, but they also provide an excellent resource for entertainment and relief of doggie tensions. Nylabone® products give your dog something to do for an hour or two every day and during that hour or two, your dog will be taking an active part in keeping his teeth and gums healthy…without even realizing it! That's invaluable to your dog, and valuable to you!

Nylabone® provides fun bones, challenging bones, and *safe* bones. It is an owner's responsibility to recognize safe chew toys from dangerous ones. Your dog will chew and devour anything you give him. Dogs must not be permitted to chew on items that they can break. Pieces of broken objects can do internal damage to a dog, besides ripping the dog's mouth. Cheap plastic or rubber toys can cause stoppage in the intestines; such stoppages are operable only if caught immediately.

The most obvious choices, in this case, may be the worst choice. Natural beef bones were not designed for chewing and cannot take too much pressure from the sides. Due to the abrasive nature of these bones, they should be offered most sparingly. Knuckle bones, though once very popular for dogs, can be easily

Nylabone® is the only plastic dog bone made of 100% virgin nylon, specially processed to create a tough, durable, completely safe bone.

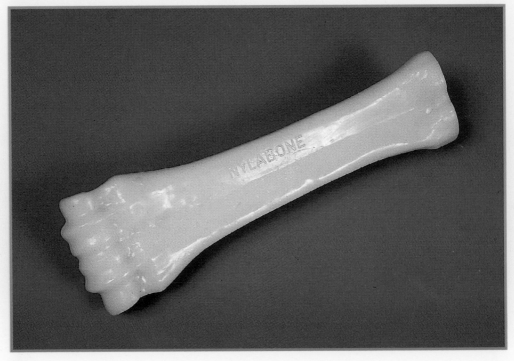

Chick-n-Cheez Chooz® are completely safe and nutritious health chews made from pure cheese protein, chicken, and fortified with vitamin E. They contain no salt, sugar, plastic, or preservatives and less than 1% fat.

chewed up and eaten by dogs. At the very least, digestion is interrupted; at worst, the dog can choke or suffer from intestinal blockage.

When a dog chews hard on a Nylabone®, little bristle-like projections appear on the surface of the bone. These help to clean the dog's teeth and add to the gum-massaging. Given the chemistry of the nylon, the bristle can pass through the dog's intestinal tract without effect. Since nylon is inert, no microorganism can grow on it, and it can be washed in soap and water or sterilized in boiling water or in an autoclave.

For the sake of your dog, his teeth and your own peace of mind, provide your dog with Nylabones®. They have 100 variations from which to choose.

FIGHTING FLEAS

Fleas are very mobile and may be red, black, or brown in color. The adults suck the blood of the host, while the larvae feed on the feces of the adults, which is rich in blood. Flea "dirt" may be seen on the pup as very tiny clusters of blackish specks that look like freshly ground pepper. The eggs of fleas may be laid on the puppy, though they are more commonly laid off the host in a favorable place, such as the bedding. They normally hatch in 4 to 21 days, depending on the temperature, but they can survive for up to 18 months if temperature conditions are not favorable. The larvae are maggot-like and molt a couple of times before forming pupae, which can survive long periods until the temperature, or the vibration of a nearby host, causes them to emerge and jump on a host.

There are a number of effective treatments available, and you should discuss them with your veterinarian, then follow all instructions for the one you choose. Any treatment will involve a product for your puppy or dog and one for the environment, and will require diligence on your part to treat all areas and thoroughly clean your home and yard until the infestation is eradicated.

THE TROUBLE WITH TICKS

Ticks are arthropods of the spider family, which means they have eight legs (though the larvae have six). They bury their headparts into the host and gorge on its blood. They are easily seen as small grain-like creatures sticking out from the skin. They are often picked up when dogs play in fields, but may also arrive in your yard via wild animals—even birds—or stray cats and dogs. Some ticks are species-specific, others are more adaptable and will host on many species.

The cat flea is the most common flea of dogs. It starts feeding soon after it makes contact with the dog.

The deer tick is the most common carrier of Lyme disease. Photo courtesy of Virbac Laboratories, Inc., Fort Worth, Texas.

The most troublesome type of tick is the deer tick, which spreads the deadly Lyme disease that can cripple a dog (or a person). Deer ticks are tiny and very hard to detect. Often, by the time they're big enough to notice, they've been feeding on the dog for a few days—long enough to do their damage. Lyme disease was named for the area of the United States in which it was first detected—Lyme, Connecticut—but has now been diagnosed in almost all parts of the U.S. Your veterinarian can advise you of the danger to your dog(s) in your area, and may suggest your dog be vaccinated for Lyme. Always go over your dog with a fine-toothed flea comb when you come in from walking through any area that may harbor deer ticks, and if your dog is acting unusually sluggish or sore, seek veterinary advice.

Attempts to pull a tick free will invariably leave the headpart in the pup, where it will die and cause an infected wound or abscess. The best way to remove ticks is to dab a strong saline solution, iodine, or alcohol on them. This will numb them, causing them to loosen their hold, at which time they can be removed with forceps. The wound can then be cleaned and covered with an antiseptic ointment. If ticks are common in your area, consult with your vet for a suitable pesticide to be used in kennels, on bedding, and on the puppy or dog.

INSECTS AND OTHER OUTDOOR DANGERS

There are many biting insects, such as mosquitoes, that can cause discomfort to a puppy. Many diseases are transmitted by the males of these species.

A pup can easily get a grass seed or thorn lodged between his pads or in the folds of his ears. These may go unnoticed until an abscess forms.

This is where your daily check of the puppy or dog will do a world of good. If your puppy has been playing in long grass or places where there may be thorns, pine needles, wild animals, or parasites, the check-up is a wise precaution.

After a romp outdoors, be sure to check your Field Spaniel's coat for fleas and ticks. Ch. Calico's So Fine Four-O-Nine, UDX, owned by the author.

SKIN DISORDERS

Apart from problems associated with lesions created by biting pests, a puppy may fall foul to a number of other skin disorders. Examples are ringworm, mange, and eczema. Ringworm is not caused by a worm, but is a fungal infection. It manifests itself as a sore-looking bald circle. If your puppy should have any form of bald patches, let your veterinarian check him over; a microscopic examination can confirm the condition. Many old remedies for ringworm exist, such as iodine, carbolic acid, formalin, and other tinctures, but modern drugs are superior.

Fungal infections can be very difficult to treat, and even more difficult to eradicate, because of the spores. These can withstand most treatments, other than burning, which is the best thing to do with bedding once the condition has been confirmed.

Mange is a general term that can be applied to many skin conditions where the hair falls out and a flaky crust develops and falls away.

Often, dogs will scratch themselves, and this invariably is worse than the original condition, for it opens lesions that are then subject to viral, fungal, or parasitic attack. The cause of the problem can be various species of mites. These either live on skin debris and the hair follicles, which they destroy, or they bury themselves just beneath the skin and feed on the tissue. Applying general remedies from pet stores is not recommended because it is essential to identify the type of mange before a specific treatment is effective.

Eczema is another non-specific term applied to many skin disorders. The condition can be brought about in many ways. Sunburn, chemicals, allergies to foods, drugs, pollens, and even stress can all produce a deterioration of the skin and coat. Given the range of causal factors, treatment can be difficult because the problem is one of identification. It is a case of taking each possibility at a time and trying to correctly diagnose the matter. If the cause is of a dietary nature then you must remove one item at a time in order to find out if the dog is allergic to a given food. It could, of course, be the lack of a nutrient that is the problem, so if the condition persists, you should consult your veterinarian.

INTERNAL DISORDERS

It cannot be overstressed that it is very foolish to attempt to diagnose an internal disorder without the advice of a veterinarian. Take a relatively common problem such as diarrhea. It might be caused by nothing more serious than the puppy hogging a lot of food or eating something that it has never previously eaten. Conversely, it could be the first indication of a potentially fatal disease. It's up to your veterinarian to make the correct diagnosis.

The following symptoms, especially if they accompany each other or are progressively added to earlier symptoms, mean you should visit the veterinarian right away:

Continual vomiting. All dogs vomit from time to time and this is not necessarily a sign of illness. They will eat grass to induce vomiting. It is a natural cleansing process common to many carnivores. However, continued vomiting is a clear sign of a problem. It may be a blockage in the pup's intestinal tract, it may be induced by worms, or it could be due to any number of diseases.

Diarrhea. This, too, may be nothing more than a temporary condition due to many factors. Even a change of home can induce diarrhea, because this often stresses the pup, and invariably there is some change in the diet. If it persists more than 48 hours then something is amiss. If blood is seen in the feces, waste no time at all in taking the dog to the vet.

Running eyes and/or nose. A pup might have a chill and this will cause the eyes and nose to weep. Again, this should quickly clear up if the puppy is placed in a warm environment and away from any drafts. If it does not, and especially if a mucous discharge is seen, then the pup has an illness that must be diagnosed.

Coughing. Prolonged coughing is a sign of a problem, usually of a respiratory nature.

Wheezing. If the pup has difficulty breathing and makes a wheezing sound when breathing, then something is wrong.

Cries when attempting to defecate or urinate. This might only be a minor problem due to the hard state of the feces, but it could be more serious, especially if the pup cries when urinating.

Cries when touched. Obviously, if you do not handle a puppy with care he might yelp. However, if he cries even when lifted gently, then he has an internal problem that becomes apparent when pressure is applied to a given area of the body. Clearly, this must be diagnosed.

Refuses food. Generally, puppies and dogs are greedy creatures when it comes to feeding time. Some might be more fussy, but none should refuse more than one meal. If they go for a number of hours without showing any interest in their food, then something is not as it should be.

General listlessness. All puppies have their off days when they do not seem their usual cheeky, mischievous selves. If this condition persists for more than two days then there is little doubt of a problem. They may not show any of the signs listed, other than perhaps a reduced interest in their food. There are many diseases that can develop internally without displaying obvious clinical signs. Blood, fecal, and other tests are needed in order to identify the disorder before it reaches an advanced state that may not be treatable.

WORMS

There are many species of worms, and a number of these live in the tissues of dogs and most other animals. Many create no problem at all, so you are not even aware they exist. Others can be tolerated in small levels, but become a major problem if they number more than a few. The most common types seen in dogs are roundworms and tapeworms. While roundworms are the greater problem, tapeworms require an intermediate host so are more easily eradicated.

Roundworms are spaghetti-like worms that cause a pot-bellied appearance and dull coat, along with more severe symptoms, such as diarrhea and vomiting. Photo courtesy of Merck AgVet.

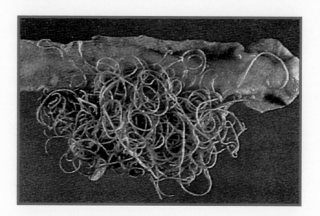

Roundworms of the species *Toxocara canis* infest the dog. They may grow to a length of 8 inches (20 cm) and look like strings of spaghetti. The worms feed on the digesting food in the pup's intestines. In chronic cases the puppy will become pot-bellied, have diarrhea, and will vomit. Eventually, he will stop eating, having passed through the stage when he always seems hungry. The worms lay eggs in the puppy and these pass out in his feces. They are then either ingested by the pup, or they are eaten by mice, rats, or beetles. These may then be eaten by the puppy and the life cycle is complete.

Larval worms can migrate to the womb of a pregnant bitch, or to her mammary glands, and this is how they pass to the puppy. The pregnant bitch can be wormed, which will help. The pups can, and should,

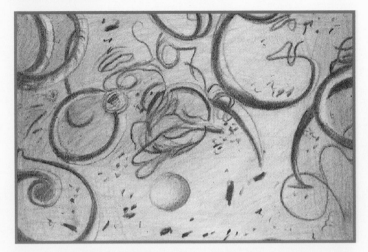

Whipworms are hard to find unless you strain your dog's feces, and this is best left to a veterinarian. Pictured here are adult whipworms.

be wormed when they are about two weeks old. Repeat worming every 10 to 14 days and the parasites should be removed. Worms can be extremely dangerous to young puppies, so you should be sure the pup is wormed as a matter of routine.

Tapeworms can be seen as tiny rice-like eggs sticking to the puppy's or dog's anus. They are less destructive, but still undesirable. The eggs are eaten by mice, fleas, rabbits, and other animals that serve as intermediate hosts. They develop into a larval stage and the host must be eaten by the dog in order to complete the chain. Your vet will supply a suitable remedy if tapeworms are seen or suspected. There are other worms, such as hookworms and whipworms, that are also blood suckers. They will make a pup anemic, and blood might be seen in the feces, which can be examined by the vet to confirm their presence. Cleanliness in all matters is the best preventative measure for all worms.

Heartworm infestation in dogs is passed by mosquitoes but can be prevented by a monthly (or daily) treatment that is given orally. Talk to your veterinarian about the risk of heartworm in your area.

BLOAT (GASTRIC DILATATION)

This condition has proved fatal in many dogs, especially large and deep-chested breeds, such as the Weimaraner and the Great Dane. However, any dog can get bloat. It is caused by swallowing air during exercise, food/water gulping or another strenuous task. As many believe, it is not the result of flatulence. The stomach of an affected dog twists, disallowing food and blood flow and resulting in harmful toxins being released into the bloodstream. Death can easily follow if the condition goes undetected.

The best preventative measure is not to feed large meals or exercise your puppy or dog immediately after he has eaten. Veterinarians recommend feeding three smaller meals per day in an elevated feeding rack, adding water to dry food to prevent gulping, and not offering water during mealtimes.

VACCINATIONS

Every puppy, purebred or mixed breed, should be vaccinated against the major canine diseases. These are distemper, leptospirosis, hepatitis, and canine parvovirus. Your puppy may have received a temporary vaccination against distemper before you purchased him, but be sure to ask the breeder to be sure.

The age at which vaccinations are given can vary, but will usually be when the pup is 8 to 12 weeks old. By this time any protection given to the pup by antibodies received from his mother via her initial milk feeds will be losing their strength.

Rely on your veterinarian for the most effectual vaccination schedule for your Field Spaniel puppy.

The puppy's immune system works on the basis that the white blood cells engulf and render harm-

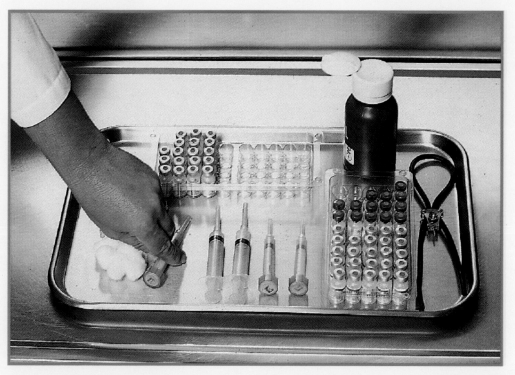

less attacking bacteria. However, they must first recognize a potential enemy.

Vaccines are either dead bacteria or they are live, but in very small doses. Either type prompts the pup's defense system to attack them. When a large attack then comes (if it does), the immune system recognizes it and massive numbers of lymphocytes (white blood corpuscles) are mobilized to counter the attack. However, the ability of the cells to recognize these dangerous viruses can diminish over a period of time. It is therefore useful to provide annual reminders about the nature of the enemy. This is done by means of booster injections that keep the immune system on its alert. Immunization is not 100-percent guaranteed to be successful, but is very close. Certainly it is better than giving the puppy no protection.

Dogs are subject to other viral attacks, and if these are of a high-risk factor in your area, then your vet will suggest you have the puppy vaccinated against these as well.

Your puppy or dog should also be vaccinated against the deadly rabies virus. In fact, in many places it is illegal for your dog not to be vaccinated. This is to protect your dog, your family, and the rest of the animal population from this deadly virus that infects the nervous system and causes dementia and death.

ACCIDENTS

All puppies will get their share of bumps and bruises due to the rather energetic way they play. These will usually heal themselves over a few days. Small cuts should be bathed with a suitable disinfectant and then smeared with an antiseptic ointment. If a cut looks more serious, then stem the flow of blood with a towel or makeshift tourniquet and rush the pup to the veterinarian. Never apply so much pressure to the wound that it might restrict the flow of blood to the limb.

In the case of burns you should apply cold water or an ice pack to the surface. If the burn was due to a chemical, then this must be washed away with copious amounts of water. Apply petroleum jelly, or any vegetable oil, to the burn. Trim away the hair if need be. Wrap the dog in a blanket and rush him to the vet. The pup may go into shock, depending on the severity of the burn, and this will result in a lowered blood pressure, which is dangerous and the reason the pup must receive immediate veterinary attention.

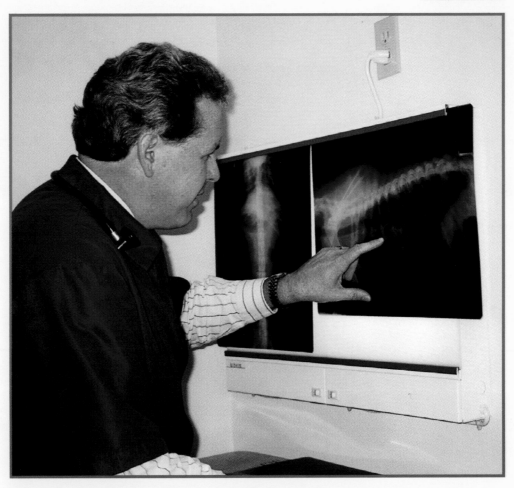

It is a good idea to x-ray the chest and abdomen on any dog hit by a car.

If a broken limb is suspected then try to keep the animal as still as possible. Wrap your pup or dog in a blanket to restrict movement and get him to the veterinarian as soon as possible. Do not move the dog's head so it is tilting backward, as this might result in blood entering the lungs.

Do not let your pup jump up and down from heights, as this can cause considerable shock to the joints. Like all youngsters, puppies do not know when enough is enough, so you must do all their thinking for them.

Provided you apply strict hygiene to all aspects of raising your puppy, and you make daily checks on his physical state, you have done as much as you can to safeguard him during his most vulnerable period. Routine visits to your veterinarian are also recommended, especially while the puppy is under one year of age. The vet may notice something that did not seem important to you.

MUZZLE

EYES

SKULL

NOSE

EARS

FEATHERING

FORELEGS

PASTERN

Ch. Bitterblue's Triple Crown, WDX, CGC, TDI, owned by Terry and Sharon Deputy, Lynn G. Finney, and Helga Alderfer.